T0044913

Exposed

Exposed

How Revealing Your Data and Eliminating Privacy Increases Trust and Liberates Humanity

Ben Malisow

WILEY

Copyright © 2021 by John Wiley & Sons, Inc., Indianapolis, Indiana

Published simultaneously in Canada

ISBN: 978-1-119-74163-3
ISBN: 978-1-119-74168-8 (ebk)
ISBN: 978-1-119-74167-1 (ebk)

Manufactured in the United States of America

No part of this publication may be reproduced, stored in a retrieval system or transmitted in any form or by any means, electronic, mechanical, photocopying, recording, scanning or otherwise, except as permitted under Sections 107 or 108 of the 1976 United States Copyright Act, without either the prior written permission of the Publisher, or authorization through payment of the appropriate per-copy fee to the Copyright Clearance Center, 222 Rosewood Drive, Danvers, MA 01923, (978) 750-8400, fax (978) 646-8600. Requests to the Publisher for permission should be addressed to the Permissions Department, John Wiley & Sons, Inc., 111 River Street, Hoboken, NJ 07030, (201) 748-6011, fax (201) 748-6008, or online at www.wiley.com/go/permissions.

Limit of Liability/Disclaimer of Warranty: The publisher and the author make no representations or warranties with respect to the accuracy or completeness of the contents of this work and specifically disclaim all warranties, including without limitation warranties of fitness for a particular purpose. No warranty may be created or extended by sales or promotional materials. The advice and strategies contained herein may not be suitable for every situation. This work is sold with the understanding that the publisher is not engaged in rendering legal, accounting, or other professional services. If professional assistance is required, the services of a competent professional person should be sought. Neither the publisher nor the author shall be liable for damages arising herefrom. The fact that an organization or Web site is referred to in this work as a citation and/or a potential source of further information does not mean that the author or the publisher endorses the information the organization or website may provide or recommendations it may make. Further, readers should be aware that Internet websites listed in this work may have changed or disappeared between when this work was written and when it is read.

For general information on our other products and services please contact our Customer Care Department within the United States at (877) 762-2974, outside the United States at (317) 572-3993 or fax (317) 572-4002.

Wiley publishes in a variety of print and electronic formats and by print-on-demand. Some material included with standard print versions of this book may not be included in e-books or in print-on-demand. If this book refers to media such as a CD or DVD that is not included in the version you purchased, you may download this material at booksupport.wiley.com. For more information about Wiley products, visit www.wiley.com.

Library of Congress Control Number: 2020945327

Trademarks: Wiley and the Wiley logo are trademarks or registered trademarks of John Wiley & Sons, Inc. and/or its affiliates, in the United States and other countries, and may not be used without written permission. All other trademarks are the property of their respective owners. John Wiley & Sons, Inc. is not associated with any product or vendor mentioned in this book.

SKY10021680_101220

For my dad, Steve Malisow.
Maybe now he'll stop asking, "Oh, is this one dedicated to your
handsome, smart, wonderful father?" every time I write something.
Yes. It is. Shut up, already.

—Ben

About the Author

Ben Malisow has worked in the fields of education/training, communication, information technology, and security, and/or some combination of these industries, for more than 25 years. Prior to his current position, Mr. Malisow provided information security consulting services and training to a diverse host of clients, including the Defense Advanced Research Projects Agency (DARPA), the Department of Homeland Security (at TSA), and the FBI. He has also served as an Air Force officer, after graduating from the Air Force Academy.

An experienced trainer, Mr. Malisow has been an adjunct professor of English at the College of Southern Nevada, a computer teacher for troubled junior/senior high school students in Las Vegas, a senior instructor for the University of Texas – San Antonio, and a teacher of computer security certification prep classes for Carnegie-Mellon University's CERT/SEI.

Mr. Malisow has published widely in many fields. His latest books are *The CCSP (ISC)² Official Study Guide*, *The CCSP (ISC)² Practice Tests*, and *How to Pass Your INFOSEC Exam* from Amazon Direct. Updates to his work and his podcast, "The Sensuous Sounds of INFOSEC," can be found at securityzed.com.

Acknowledgments

There are so many people who helped in the development and refinement of this book; I want to take the opportunity to thank them all:

Kevin Galvan, for research and references.

Brian Hafter and Maren Calvert, for legal wizardry.

I must also thank Her Splendiferous Majesty Colonel Mo Barrett, USAF (ret), my classmate from the Air Force Academy, who reviewed some of the material and offered her invaluable insight on the tone and approach.

My preview readers, who gave valuable personal perspective into how each chapter resonated: Curchel Smoot, Wes Miller, Sergio Silva, Dallas Bishoff, Jonathan Aluveaux, Mike Beedlow, Tom Allen, Derek Osborne, Haider Sousa, and Stephen Villere.

Sebastian Kilchert helped verify some information for me.

Kelly Talbot, the editor who exceeds any sane description of what that position should reasonably entail; without him, many readers (and writers) would not even end up with the book they wanted (and were looking for). I am somewhat convinced Kelly is some kind of sorcerer with an advanced degree in psychology.

Jim Minatel . . . . Jim is a publisher so therefore the mortal enemy of all writers. We usually communicate by lobbing heavy glassware at each other. However, when he told me he wanted me to write this book, he did something I didn't realize publishers knew how to do: he made a writer *happy*. I can't thank him enough for the opportunity.

And Robin Cabe, who helped with pretty much all of it, including reading the whole thing before it was ready.

Contents at a Glance

Contents

Introduction

"Any sufficiently advanced technology is indistinguishable from magic."

Arthur C. Clarke

The idea of privacy is that each human being should be able to decide who has information about them. It's an interesting concept: each person creating an island of data and limiting access to the island only to other entities the individual permits.

In practice, it doesn't work, meaning it's both impossible and incredibly harmful to everyone when privacy "rights" are imposed and enforced. This is true for a number of reasons, including human nature, modern technology, and the way data functions and affects interaction.

Today, many people say they want privacy—that they value control of their own information. There is an almost innate, reflexive horror at the idea that someone, anyone, could know something about us that we did not want them to know. Many of us do not feel comfortable with this idea: what if you had no privacy—what if everything you ever did or said was known to everyone else? Each of us may have a different image of the form of that discomfort. Who knows everything about me—the government? Corporations? My spouse? And what would they do with that information? Harm me? Track me? Sell things to me? When we conceive of a dystopia, fictional or real, that depiction usually includes some aspect of loss of personal privacy, from the Big Brother intrusive government of George Orwell's *1984* (the archetypical dystopia)[1] to modern North Korean governmental control of its citizens[2] to the constant and ubiquitous monitoring of our online activity by the behemoths of the Internet, from Google to Facebook to Apple to Amazon.[3] We fear anyone that has the totality of information; if someone knows everything about me, maybe they can control me. I, myself, prize my privacy and loathe the notion that someone else knows something about me that I did not want them to know.

---

[1]Orwell, G. (1955). 1984. New York: New American Library

[2]www.hrw.org/world-report/2019/country-chapters/north-korea#

[3]abcnews.go.com/Technology/ceos-amazon-apple-facebook-google-face-congressional-antitrust/story?id=72034939

And yet . . . we want to know everything about everyone else. We are naturally curious—no, not curious: nosy. We crave gossip and innuendo and accusations; we want to know what happened and when and to whom. We have entire industries thriving on the practice of gathering, analyzing, and distributing information about other people for our consumption.[4] [5] [6] [7] [8] [9] [10] This desire runs exactly counter to our claim that privacy is important, or, at least, it suggests that we want privacy for ourselves, but nobody else.

But what if there was no privacy, for anyone or anything, at all? What if everyone knew everything about everyone else?

Imagine if you could view video from every camera in the world . . . could listen in on every microphone . . . could view every person's browser feed . . . could watch every satellite feed . . . in real time, unadulterated, any time. But also imagine that every other person had the same ability: your neighbor, your parents, your kids, your co-workers, your friends, and total strangers. What if we could all access every piece of data, live or recorded, at will?

In this book, I'm going to make the case that a world without privacy would be the optimum outcome: all data, everywhere, known to everyone. It's disconcerting; on a very personal level, I don't like the feeling I get when I consider this idea, and I think most people feel the same way. But, rationally, using objective reason instead of emotional reaction, it makes much more sense than the ultimate (unobtainable) goal of every individual having total control of information, and it is absolutely preferable to the bizarre patchwork of information disparity we currently have, where certain people and institutions have access to particular information, others have access to different sets of information, and each individual person has only limited glimpses of the whole.

---

[4] www.tmz.com
[5] people.com
[6] starmagazine.com
[7] marketingplatform.google.com/about/enterprise [formerly DoubleClick]
[8] www.cambridgeanalytica.org
[9] www.lexisnexis.com/en-us/products/public-records.page
[10] www.equifax.com/personal

The Purpose of Privacy

To begin with, it's good to dissect why this idea makes us feel uncomfortable. Why do we want (or think we want or say we want) privacy? For the most part, we think privacy will give us security; the two words are often used together, sometimes mistakenly synonymously. For most of my life, I have worked in industries where the collection, distribution, and protection of information was valuable: the military, journalism, teaching, and computer security. For security practitioners, one of the fundamental premises is called the *Triad* of security goals: confidentiality, integrity, and availability.[11]

- **Confidentiality:** Only authorized people can get access.
- **Integrity:** Only authorized transactions are allowed.
- **Availability:** The asset exists when authorized people are authorized to make transactions.

From this perspective, privacy is usually perceived as an aspect of confidentiality; individual people want control of the confidentiality of information that identifies them. And confidentiality isn't used just for personal privacy; it's used to secure data and assets in all types of activities, organizations, and business. We've depended on confidentiality as part of our effort to attain security for so long that it's hard to imagine being secure without it; it's a cornerstone of the security profession.

But it's not necessary. In fact, confidentiality often inhibits security.

For example, one of the desires we have about privacy is to protect ourselves financially—we don't want anyone else knowing our bank account information or the credentials we use to access the account (passwords, identification cards, bits of information like name and address and birthdate, etc.). Banks spend a lot of money protecting these credentials,[12] and we expend effort creating and maintaining them. All of this effort has a financial cost, which negatively impacts the financial benefit of the process and investment. Every amount the bank spends on securing the transaction is an amount charged to the customer, either through direct fees or in reduced interest on the investment—you would

---

[11]www.elsevier.com/books/the-basics-of-information-security/andress/978-0-12-800744-0

[12]www.americanbanker.com/articles/financial-firms-to-further-increase-cybersecurity-spending

make more money with your account if security wasn't an additional cost of the process. This is all to prevent fraudulent transactions—someone pretending to be you in order to get your money.

But this can happen only because the *criminal* has privacy. If all of the information about all of the transactions, legitimate and fraudulent, is known to everyone, then there is no opportunity for theft. If the bank knew when someone other than you tried to take your money, the bank would not give the money to that person. *If every action of every person is known to every other person, no transaction fraud could exist.* A criminal can't engage in theft by fraud if we all know what the criminal is doing and who the criminal is.

Total transparency, then, directly counters the need for confidentiality . . . and improves the lives of everyone involved, because we no longer have the costs associated with the need for confidentiality, and we can all then derive the greater benefits.

Going to Extremes

Take this to an even greater extreme and get weird with it: why do we even have banks? Again, it's a perceived need for security, based on money. We put our money in a bank so that someone else doesn't take our money without our permission. But . . . if everyone knows everything about everyone else, we would know if someone without permission took money from someone else. We would know if a crime was committed, and we would know who the rightful owner of the money is. The need for banks would be greatly diminished or dissipate altogether . . . and the cost of banking would similarly evaporate, and each individual person would get greater value from their own money.[13]

If what I'm describing is starting to make you feel uncomfortable and the idea of everyone watching your every action is creeping you out, that's understandable and completely normal. I'm not trying to describe a police state where you're being watched by law enforcement every moment of every day. Forget the *how* of this proposal for the moment; I'll get into theoretical mechanisms for achieving these goals throughout the book. (And, to be clear, I do not have a comprehensive way of accomplishing these goals. Putting these theories into practice

---

[13]Granted, banks provide services other than protecting savings, such as commercial/ residential loans and currency exchange.

will require the contribution and coordination of many experts, organizations, and thinkers. This book is intended to be a catalyst to start that conversation. But I think the discussion in society about privacy thus far has been overwhelmingly one-sided: everyone seems to be pursuing ways to implement and mandate more privacy, not less, as a means to ensure security. I think they're mistaken.)

It's worth noting that some jurisdictions (some cultures, some populations) value privacy in different ways. For instance, the European Union, right now, has decided that personal privacy is a human right, tantamount to living; this is codified and mandated by the General Data Protection Regulation (GDPR), which gives some power to individuals in terms of imposing who can or cannot disseminate their personal data.[14] This law also gives an even greater amount of power to the governments of the European Union, as enforcers acting on behalf of the individuals they supposedly protect. This law is mimicked around the world; similar statutes exist in countries such as Japan,[15] Switzerland,[16] Australia,[17] Canada,[18] Argentina,[19] Singapore,[20] Israel,[21] and others, as well as the American states of California[22] and New York.[23]

NOTE In government, healthcare, technology, and other fields, personal data is often referred to as *personally identifiable information* (PII). PII generally includes each person's name, address, date of birth, mobile phone number, the logical and physical addresses of their computer/device (the IP and MAC addresses), government-issued ID numbers (such as social security, driver's license, and passport numbers), and more. Privacy laws vary by jurisdiction, so what is defined as PII in one location may not be considered PII in another.

---

[14]General Data Protection Regulation, OJ L 119, 04.05.2016 § (EU) 2016/679 (2018)

[15]iapp.org/news/a/gdpr-matchup-japans-act-on-the-protection-of-personal-information

[16]www.admin.ch/opc/en/classified-compilation/19920153/index.html

[17]www.oaic.gov.au/privacy/the-privacy-act

[18]www.priv.gc.ca/en/privacy-topics/privacy-laws-in-canada/the-personal-information-protection-and-electronic-documents-act-pipeda

[19]servicios.infoleg.gob.ar/infolegInternet/anexos/60000-64999/64790/texact.htm

[20]www.pdpc.gov.sg

[21]www.gov.il/en/Departments/the_privacy_protection_authority

[22]leginfo.legislature.ca.gov/faces/billTextClient.xhtml?bill_id=201720180AB375

[23]www.dos.ny.gov/coog/pppl.html

Other jurisdictions, on the other hand, have laws and practices that are in direct opposition to personal privacy. China, for instance, has laws that require that the government have access to all online activity, including the ability to monitor the action/communication of each individual.[24] In the same vein as the European Union's justification for the GDPR, China's rationale for monitoring is to protect the citizenry. But unlike the EU, which purports to protect individual privacy, China's stated intent is a different excuse for police powers: Chinese authorities want to protect society from criminals who operate in secret or prevent disruption of society that might result because of "bad" information or influence.

Meanwhile, in the United States, prevailing national law runs exactly counter to the very idea of privacy: instead of each individual having an absolute right to privacy, each individual has an absolute right to free expression. This is codified in the US Constitution and in the First Amendment (twice, in fact, as both the freedom to say what you want and the freedom to distribute/publicize what you say—freedom of speech and freedom of the press).[25] So instead of you telling me what I can say about you, I can say anything I want about you, to anyone or everyone. That applies regardless of whether "you" means an individual, a government, or a corporation. Perhaps not surprisingly, this approach of freedom of speech, combined with transparency, will be most in line with the argument for improving the human world I'll make throughout this book.

Please Indulge Me

I'm going to ask for your indulgence as you read the rest of the book. It might seem, in a few places, that I'm suggesting that a police state is somehow preferable to personal privacy—that is definitely not the case. In fact, I think it is much more likely that privacy laws create a situation for a police state to grow and flourish. I prefer personal, individual freedom over all other things. It might also seem like what I'm describing is science fiction—that what it would take to achieve total transparency is impossible. I ask you to momentarily suspend your disbelief for the

---

[24]www.chinalawblog.com/2019/09/chinas-new-cybersecurity-program-no-place-to-hide.html

[25]www.law.cornell.edu/constitution/first_amendment

purpose of this discussion and examine the topic objectively, from the perspective of the desired end-state, and not the complications of the possible implementations.

Finally, it's probably best we all agree that there is no actual privacy (or that there probably never really was): someone knows everything about you. Not that any one person knows all the things—but all the people who know things about you could get together and assemble all that data and nothing you've done or said would be private anymore. Someone, somewhere, singly or collectively, has all of it—whether that someone is the government, corporations, or trusted loved ones, you have no privacy. You have an illusion of privacy, or the faux privacy of anonymity. These are not worth the expense and cost that the false benefit of "privacy" supposedly provides.

Premises

Secrecy is not security; confidentiality is only one leg of the Triad. If other legs of the Triad are violated/abrogated, we can lose security just as easily as if we lost confidentiality. Privacy is not security—but we often think privacy will give us security. Privacy requires secrecy; if you cannot enforce confidentiality, you have no privacy.

In the rest of this book, I'm going to describe ways that privacy and secrecy hinder actual security, or how security (whether attained through confidentiality, integrity, or availability) can harm people. It's important to understand that what we say we want, or what we think we want, is not something that is actually beneficial or useful (or at least as not as beneficial/useful as we think, especially compared to other choices). Privacy is not a magical solution to perceived problems, and privacy might actually cost each of us more than the potential benefits it provides. We might all benefit more, as individuals, from security methods other than limiting access to our own data islands. And other approaches would not incur the costs privacy requires.

Another premise: to properly discuss privacy, we need to discuss adult topics, because we, as people, usually want privacy for adult reasons (financial, sexual relationships/activity, death, business, etc.). This book will deal with those topics in frank and adult terminology—if you're uncomfortable with adult conversation, you may find parts of the book uncomfortable.

Finally, while reading the rest of the book, try to imagine that each person on the planet has a magical capacity to view and hear everyone else on the planet: a television set that can be instantly tuned to any other person, anywhere, that not only displays real-time data, but all prior activity—all historical actions and speech of every other person.

I'm not using this premise because I'm excited about the potential; from the perspective of someone who was raised in a culture that respected privacy and someone who has been engaged in the practice of security in one way or another for most of my adult life, this premise seems awkward, intrusive, dangerous, and makes me very uncomfortable.

But my personal feelings/biases don't matter: I also realize that the future I'm describing is almost here, and that it is inevitable. While I'm not relishing its arrival, I'm trying to view it as objectively as possible, and I anticipate the pitfalls and predict the opportunities. I know the situation that brings me discomfort is upon us, and I know that we can exacerbate the danger and difficulty of the transition from a private world to the post-privacy world, if we approach it with obsolete tools and philosophies.

And that magical TV set is just a step away from what we have right now—and it's only magical in Arthur C. Clarke's sense of technological sophistication. It would be better if we could start figuring out how to use our next magical tool instead of pretending it will never arrive.

How to Contact the Publisher

If you believe you've found a mistake in this book, please bring it to our attention. At John Wiley & Sons, we understand how important it is to provide our customers with accurate content, but even with our best efforts an error may occur.

To submit your possible errata, please email it to our Customer Service Team at wileysupport@wiley.com with the subject line "Possible Book Errata Submission."

1

Privacy Cases: Being Suborned

"Well . . . how did I get here?"
—*David Byrne, "Once in a Lifetime"*

To discuss the relative merits of personal privacy, it's worth reviewing historic rationales and justifications for security processes and programs. Privacy and security have become linked to the point where the ideas are almost inextricable, and it is valuable to understand how this came to happen.

Security Through Trust

One of the concepts that relates to privacy is security through trust— an institution, government, or company is considered more trustworthy if the personnel working in or for it are themselves trustworthy. To determine whether a person is trustworthy, it's important to learn certain things about the person: their behavior, tendencies, condition, mindset, and so forth. Trust is established based on past performance; we tend to believe that someone will act more or less in a manner similar to how they already have. The assumption is: a lying junkie will continue to be a lying junkie; a person who has worked diligently and honorably for their entire adult life will continue to behave diligently and honorably. There are, of course, outliers and changes in circumstance where predictions are wildly unhinged from the past; the junkie might change overnight and become a paragon of virtue and a hard worker, whereas the model employee might turn into a depraved murderer in a moment. Human beings are fickle, unpredictable, irrational creatures. But if you have to trust someone, you will generally tend to use their past actions as an indicator for what you expect of them in the future.

The Historic Trust Model Creates Oppression

Not so long ago, many organizations had some rather bizarre criteria programmed into their trust models—metrics that we would find ridiculous, offensive, stupid, and/or downright evil today. These have included gender, race, religion, ethnicity, and national origin.

For instance, at the outset of World War II, American President Roosevelt considered people of Japanese descent, including American citizens with Japanese parents and grandparents, untrustworthy, to the point where he believed they might aid Japan in its war against the United States. He therefore ordered them to be forced into concentration camps.[1] The rationale was: this would make the United States more secure. Personal privacy, in that circumstance, was not an aspect of the trust model; significant physiognomic traits, combined with birth and immigration records, allowed the US government to enforce this horrible decision. There was not much room for question as to the ethnicity of the prisoners.

Privately Trustful

Another awful aspect of the personnel trust model was, however, larger a facet of what is generally considered "private" life: whether that person engaged in same-gender sexual activity.

> **NOTE**   For purposes of discussion in this book, I'll use the term *gay* to mean the full spectrum of what we now often call LGBTQ—lesbian, gay, bisexual, transgender, queer—sometimes with additional descriptors.

There were two main (ugly and horribly flawed) rationalizations for this type of policy.

- Gay people are untrustworthy because of their very nature; sexual orientation is a choice, gay people engaging in sexual acts is an indicator of character, and only depraved people would choose to do so.

---

[1] Executive Order 9066. www.ourdocuments.gov/doc.php?flash=false&doc=74&page=transcript

- Gay people are untrustworthy because they are susceptible to coercion; anyone learning of a person's sexual interactions or desires could use that knowledge against the person—a gay person could be blackmailed for being gay.

The first "reason" is so tragically stupid that it's hard for people today to realize that people in the past actually believed ideas like this. It almost certainly had origins in religious and cultural biases and misanthropic tendencies tantamount to evil. The second rationale is insidious in a different way and is a perfect of example of how privacy and security can become conflated to the point of causing true harm to the very things they purportedly are meant to protect.

NOTE   At the time the laws/policies discussed in this chapter were created/implemented/enforced, there were other terms used to describe any sexual activity that did not conform to heteronormative standards, typically *unnatural acts* and *sodomy*, when included in statutes or other written mandates.

The historical personnel trust model is based on some simple premises: institutional trust is linked to personal trust, personal trust is based on using past behavior to predict future action, and personal behavior outside the workplace (such as sexual activity) is linked to personal behavior in the workplace. For the institution to trust the individual for a particular job, the institution must learn and know about the person's behavior outside the workplace, in their personal life. That's the institution's perspective.

Generally, from the individual's perspective (instead of the institution's), we like to think of a person's home life and work life as two separate, distinct contexts: I act in accordance with my employer's needs during the hours I'm working, because that's what I'm getting paid for, but when I am not working, I am free to live my life in the manner I see fit, without my employer's oversight. I might wear a uniform in the workplace, but I take it off when I'm not working; I associate with colleagues and customers while I'm working, but I might have a totally different set of friends and acquaintances when I'm not working, and I might not interact with the workplace colleagues/customers until I'm back in the workplace.

In reality, this construct often breaks down in actual practice. Colleagues and customers share information about their nonwork activities in workplace discussions, and actions a person takes outside the workplace can seriously affect their employment, be it acquiring a college degree or running someone over with a car while driving drunk. Even so, we often like to think of ourselves as having a bifurcated existence.

In order for the dated trust model, which discriminated against gay people to have existed, the institution had to breach the employee's private life—sex is generally (with very, very few exceptions) an activity that happens outside the workplace. This intrusiveness was seen as necessary in order to ensure that the person placed in a position of trust by the institution was, indeed, trustworthy.

This, of course, makes absolutely no sense, when exposed to even the barest logical scrutiny. Were gay people subject to blackmail/coercion because of their same-gender sexual activity? Yes—*but only because the institutional trust model created that situation.* The person who is given employment or promotion only under the condition that they act in a prescribed manner (or, more to the point, do not act in a proscribed manner) is under the threat of losing something of value (a job, a promotion, etc.) if their unapproved behavior becomes known.

Disarmed Forces

Here's a historic example: the US military has its own laws and court system; this is known as the Uniform Code of Military Justice (UCMJ). Not too long ago, the UCMJ prohibited same-gender sexual activity; violations could be punished with demotions, dismissal, or even imprisonment.[2] The government had similar, if more vaguely worded, restrictions in Executive Order 10450, "Security Requirements for Government Employment." In both the military and other government positions, a security clearance (the documented verification of a person's trustworthiness) was (and still is) considered extremely valuable—a person with a security clearance could get employment and other opportunities that a person without a clearance could not. A person in the military/

---

[2] Uniform Code of Military Justice, 1950. Article 125, Sodomy, Sections (a) and (b). "(a) Any person subject to this Code who engages in unnatural carnal copulation with another of the same or opposite sex or with an animal is guilty of sodomy. Penetration, however slight, is sufficient to complete the offence. (b) Any person found guilty of sodomy shall be punished as a court-martial may direct." www.loc.gov/rr/frd/Military_Law/pdf/morgan.pdf, pg. 161

government service could lose their security clearance if the military/government learned that the person was gay.[3]

So, the military/government (and institutions who had similar anti-gay policies) had created a situation where certain people had something to lose (the clearance, and the benefits that come with a clearance) if information about them (personal information, from their "private" life) was disclosed. That, therefore, put those people at risk of coercion and put the institution at risk overall (a trusted person might be coerced into causing harm to the institution). If, however, the anti-gay rules/policies did *not* exist, then the entire possibility for coercion would not exist, and trust would not be in question.

NOTE   Within reason, and taken in context, a person might not be subject to coercion *only* because of their employment status and situation, and that employer's policies—there might be other aspects of a person's life that could be used to coerce them into harming their employer. At the time the UCMJ had rules against same-gender sexual activity, there were also social mores and prejudices that might make someone gay subject to coercion as well; a blackmailer might threaten the target with outing them to their *family* as opposed to their employer and might therefore get the victim to do something harmful to the employer. "I will show these photos of you with your gay lover to your children, unless you steal these files from your office." Societal and cultural dysfunction played a large part in workplace discrimination, as well. Typically, however, the employers' rules both reflected and exacerbated the cultural norms.

Missed Application

While employer-created susceptibility to coercion was bad enough, these institutions further harmed themselves by adhering to this flawed trust model in the application and enforcement of the mandates. The rules were never applied fairly, uniformly, or sensibly; there are many notorious cases where the rules were instead used to settle personal workplace grudges, by resentful lovers/spouses/friends as revenge, for

---

[3] Executive Order 10450—"Security requirements for Government employment," 1953. www.archives.gov/federal-register/codification/executive-order/10450.html

political damage, to gain advantage by a competitor for a position/promotion, or even simply by small-minded bureaucrats insistent on following the law regardless of sense or harm to the "lawbreaker."

Here's one example of lack of uniformity/sense in applying the rules (and the trust model) regarding personal (private) behavior: a group of British men, acting as Soviet spies from the 1930s through the 1950s, known as the Cambridge Five.[4] At least two of the men were gay, and a third bisexual[5] . . . and almost all of them were known to regularly abuse alcohol, to the point where drinking significantly impacted their behavior (one of the KGB handlers of the spies noted that one of the Five, MacLean, may have revealed the fact that he was a spy to both a lover and a sibling while drunk). Yet none of them was prosecuted by the British government, although their behavior was presumably known to British authorities as well. This can be directly contrasted with the case of Alan Turing, another British government employee, whose cryptographic work is famously thought to have been instrumental in the Allied effort to win World War II. Turing was convicted of "indecency" in 1952, under the Criminal Law Amendment Act of 1885,[6] and was subjected to chemical castration as part of a sentencing arrangement; he lost his security clearance as well, which ended his consulting work with the British government and may have led to his suicide in 1954 (the details of his death do not rule out accidental causes).

Arbitrary enforcement of any law is atrocious; it degrades the rule of law and overall concepts of justice. However, with these particular laws, designed specifically to control the private lives of citizens, lack of uniformity in application creates fear, mistrust, and a horrific sense of unease and anxiety among the very people the laws are supposed to protect. Anyone who might be victimized by their own legal system is naturally terrified of this possibility. To underscore the relationship of this situation to the premise of the book: *laws designed to protect privacy necessarily create situations where there are "private" lives/data distinct from "open" lives/data, and situations where the distinction between what is known and what is not, especially by law enforcers and the*

---

[4] Editorial. (2014). Cambridge Five spy ring members 'hopeless drunks.' BBC website: www.bbc.com/news/uk-england-cambridgeshire-28143770

[5] www.bbc.com/news/magazine-35360172

[6] Criminal Law Amendment Act of 1885. www.swarb.co.uk/acts/1885Criminal_Law_AmendmentAct.shtml

individuals affected, can cause fear, mistrust, and unnecessary hardship on individuals. Moreover, even laws created with the very best of intent (and, to give the benefit of the doubt to lawmakers, let's assume that means all laws, although I certainly think there's a great deal of room to argue that point) often have unintended consequences. With privacy laws, one of the obvious, predictable, "unintended" consequences is to create sets of data that are sensitive—giving power to those people and institutions that are allowed to transcend or abrogate those laws (such as the government and law enforcement entities). A set of data that is sensitive is a set of data that can be leveraged, often to the detriment of the very citizenry who are supposed to be protected by those laws (the individuals who the data describes). Again: by creating "protected" information, we create a potential to cause harm.

Harmfully Ever After

What harms did those obsolete laws and policies, based on the atrociously flawed trust models, cause? Aside from the personal harm to each individual affected (those like Turing who lost their jobs, prominence, and respect in their fields of endeavor, and often freedom), what harm does this cause to society at large?

The first and most obvious terrible impact is the loss of potential candidates for trusted positions that become ineligible. This might happen through self-elimination—candidates who fear being identified and punished for personal actions/behaviors/beliefs therefore do not even attempt to pursue positions where they might be considered or investigated. It also includes those people who still attempt to take those positions but are turned away or rejected by the institutions as unsuitable. On top of these are the people who still sought those positions (knowing that they, themselves, could be identified, eliminated, or even prosecuted), actually achieved their intent and took those roles, but then were fired/removed from the positions later because their private lives and actions came to light.[7] Qualified, accomplished people have been removed from candidacy for those positions, or removed after a time of faithful service, and the negative impact is felt by both the institutions and the society as a whole that is served by those institutions.

---

[7] St. Martin's Press. (1993). *Conduct Unbecoming: Gays and Lesbians in the U.S. Military: Vietnam to the Persian Gulf* (1st ed.). Aurora, IL

And possibly the most terrible harm in distinguishing a "private" life from a "public" persona is creating a situation where the person in a position of trust—in a job, in their community, in their family—must always have a continuous fear, the constant knowledge that at any time their livelihood and identity could be ruined, if they were to be "outed" (that is, if someone reveals the heretofore "private" knowledge about them, without the target's consent/permission). This must be a lingering, gnawing apprehension, something that infects and degrades every success and keeps people who experience this risk from enjoying their lives fully. That is a severe cost, and a constant toll. It's one of the reasons why many laws in many jurisdictions have a statute of limitations: every perpetrator must live with the constant knowledge that they could be arrested and prosecuted at any moment, that they are hunted, and that is a form of punishment in itself.

At first pass, this might seem like a reason *for* privacy: to set up stringent distinctions between an individual's private life and their public identity. We might view as beneficial the possibility of distinguishing, for ourselves, what is revealed to others, and what is held in secret. In practice, however, this causes only opportunities for abuse, malfeasance, and fear: anything secret and distinct lends a potential for exploitation and attack—anyone with entrée to your (supposedly) private life has power over you, even if that power can only be used to hurt you.

Open Air

How would openness and an end to privacy have served as a benefit to the gay people vilified and persecuted by laws like Executive Order 10450 and the Criminal Law Amendment Act? Wouldn't the *lack* of privacy have been more damaging to the targets of those laws, denying them any opportunities for positions of trust, by not allowing them to keep their identities and behavior secret? (That is, is there an argument to be made that *having* privacy created the only opportunity for gay people to attain those positions of trust in a hostile environment?)

The answer is: if the actions of every person were known to every other person, then same-gender sexual activity (or any activity associated with gay people) would not and could not be seen as wildly deviating from the norm, nor as inherently dishonorable or disreputable, for two reasons—the significant percentage of human beings who engage in the proscribed behavior and the existence of a large number of gay people known to be eminently trustworthy.

If everyone knows that everyone else engages in a particular activity, that activity cannot reasonably be vilified . . . and even if prejudices and social mores exist that attempt to vilify the particular activity, *enforcement* cannot be meted out uniformly and evenly throughout the entire population. To wit: many laws that prohibited sodomy specifically included oral sex—if every person (hetero or otherwise) who has ever received or given a blowjob were under the same threat of prosecution and punishment, then a vast majority of the population would live in continual fear of exposure, and every person (no matter their station in life) would face the same risk . . . and when the overwhelming majority of people face equivalent risk, laws inevitably must change to alleviate their fear, if for no other reason than powerful people do not like the prospect of losing their power and will work to reduce their own risk.

Moreover, those laws prohibiting certain types of sexual behavior were based on ignorance: the presupposition that same-gender sexual activity denoted flawed character, indicating the person was somehow immoral or untrustworthy. *Actual ignorance can only exist in absence of data*—if people know, factually, that an assumption is patently incorrect, then that assumption cannot be used as a basis for law or regulation, unless that society or institution wishes to put itself in jeopardy solely in pursuit of its own superstitions. The latter case is willful ignorance—belief in something either in absence of data or counter to that evidence. If every person can see every other person's activity, including sexual acts, and it is quickly revealed that there is absolutely no correlation between a particular sexual act and trustworthiness or capability, then only someone purposefully willing to put themself or their institution at greater risk of failure would continue to act in accordance with the bias against certain actions or people.

Artifice Exemplar

I'll create a wholly artificial, philosophical construct for an example. The country of Abandonia is biased against a certain group of people (be them gay or of a certain ethnicity or religious group or whatever) and therefore prohibits individuals of that group to participate in the leadership/staff of Abandonia. The nation of Bearington does not have that same prejudice and hires the best people for leadership positions, regardless of their orientation, gender, ethnicity, religion, or other affiliation.

When Abandonia comes into direct competition with Bearington, Bearington will have a distinct advantage. There will be some people, whatever amount that might be, in the disfavored class of Abandonia who would be more capable than some people of the favored group, but Abandonia won't avail itself of their service. Bearington won't have any such compunction and will only choose and promote people based on merit. Bearington will prevail against Abandonia, because Bearington will have the best people in all positions. The generals of the army in Bearington will be more militarily capable than their counterparts in Abandonia, because those people were not chosen according to inaccurate assumptions, and Bearington will reap the benefits and defeat Abandonia over and over. Bearington will have better business leaders, civic leaders, scientists, engineers, and employees at all levels, in all endeavors . . . because no Bearingtonian will be held back by the inherent superstitions and biases that Abandonia enshrines.

Full knowledge of the merits of individual people, their trustworthiness and capabilities, exposed to all other people, forces everyone to judge everyone else on their merits, and not on the false suppositions and assumptions of irrational prejudice. Irrational prejudice can only survive in privacy. *Lack* of knowledge allows biases; biases cannot withstand hard data. *Secrecy and privacy allow unfounded prejudice—* removing secrecy and privacy diminish the hold of superstition.

In the following chapters, I offer more examples of how secrecy and confidentiality are not the bargain they appear to be, and how revealing all data, making public all information, is not the threat it appears to be . . . and, in fact, liberates us all. I will also explain the manifold benefits of universal openness: how a lack of privacy enhances humanity.

2

Privacy Cases: Government/ National Intelligence/ Military Confidentiality

"The urge to save humanity is almost always only a false-face for the urge to rule it."

—H. L. Mencken, *Minority Report*

Chapter 1 discussed examples of how governments and militaries use policies and laws to dictate which people are placed in positions of trust (and how those laws require privacy to exist and harm the institutions they're designed to protect). Chapter 2 addresses another flawed excuse for privacy: the privacy of governments, intelligence agencies, and the military. This is far different from personal privacy; this is an institutional, far-reaching kind of privacy, addressing the activities of many people and groups. I feel, however, it is extremely important to address the perceived desire for this kind of privacy in much the same way, simply because when I suggest that *all* privacy be ended, because privacy is definitely going to end for some of us there may be, for modern people, a natural apprehension and tendency to counter that these institutions must naturally be excepted, because of the nature of their design and function. That is, even if the reader might possibly be convinced that personal privacy was somehow a thing we could all do better without, they might feel that *of course* we would carve out an exception to this new paradigm, allowing governments, spy agencies, and military organizations to carry on their work in private.

I'm going to attempt to dissuade you from this perspective.

National Security vs. Governmental Security

One of the fundamental assumptions of the need for government secrecy is to protect "national security"—the premise that a nation-state could not exist without hiding information. Even on its face, this seems awkward, even distasteful. Who is the information being hidden *from*? And why is that necessary? Isn't a democracy (or really, any type of free society) predicated on openness? How can a free people choose their government without access to knowledge of how that government functions and operates? If the electorate does not know about their government, then it seems fairly basic that they are not making informed decisions . . . and then are therefore not truly free. To make a valid choice, you must be aware of what choice you're making—what options you're choosing between. Hidden information obscures your knowledge of the choices and deprives you of consent.

Instead, the phrase *national security* is used most often to mean something else, a concept we don't usually discuss or describe: governmental security. If the populace is unaware of what the government is doing, the government is allowed to act in any manner the government chooses. Lacking oversight, a government can be capricious, biased, or even evil. This can, of course, only be done with secrecy; when the people at large are aware of how the government behaves, any biases or favoritism or wrongdoing is known . . . and the government cannot long endure. Scrutiny leads to a loss of government power (or, at the least, reduces the unchecked power of the government).

Governments, obviously, are also only people. A subset of people as a whole, governments are people granted certain privileges and powers not ceded to all. Those people who are granted this power (governments) typically enjoy it; in fact, they have sought it out, and they desire to keep it. Quite often, they also want to expand the powers they have. *National security*, then, is often code for, "protecting me from losing my power." If someone else were to know about the actions of the people in power, those people might lose whatever privilege and power they'd been granted (whether that be the result of an election, prosecution, or revolution).

This is not to say that raw power is the sole motivation for all people in all governments. But every other rationale given by someone in government service boils down to that core function. For instance,

"I want to change the world for the better," does not require government mandate or authority—you can behave in any manner you believe makes the world a better place, without need for license or office to make that happen. However, people who seek the power of a government office to effect change are purposefully attempting to gain power to impose their will on other people, whether the change they seek is large or small.

A law to create a new automotive traffic ordinance uses the same mechanisms and apparatus as any other law; the person seeking political office may truly believe that the traffic ordinance can only possibly improve the world (or their little part of it), but it is political power that makes a traffic ordinance, and political power that enforces it. A traffic ordinance is upheld by law enforcers and courts: someone violating this traffic ordinance will be compelled to pay a fine; if they refuse to pay, law enforcers will physically capture and detain them; if they continue to refuse to pay, they can be incarcerated; if they refuse to be incarcerated (or initially apprehended/detained), they can be beaten or killed. All laws, all government functions, are ultimately issued at the point of a gun.

The traffic law (presumably) was not created with the intent to kill; it was created with the intent to reduce harm. Ultimately, it is only enforced through the use or threat of overwhelming power.

Obviously, there should be no need for the use of secrecy in deploying and maintaining traffic laws. If there's any situation where public transparency shouldn't be in question whatsoever, it's knowing the rationale, mechanisms, and results of traffic laws.

And here's where real life gets weird: even information about *traffic laws* has been the subject of governmental secrecy efforts.[1]

A man in Oregon published a mathematical proof that the traffic light cameras in his jurisdiction were incorrectly calculating driver behavior; when he published this proof, he cited the fact that he is an engineer. A government body in his jurisdiction imposed a fine on him, saying he was not licensed as an engineer by that jurisdiction and could not therefore use the word *engineer* in conjunction with published data. While this is not strictly an example of keeping traffic data secret, it clearly demonstrates an attempt to control how information is disseminated and presented. Theoretically, the purpose of the law against using the

---

[1] ij.org/press-release/oregon-engineer-makes-history-with-new-traffic-light-timing-formula

word *engineer* is to reduce the possibility that consumers of engineering services could be deceived by uncredentialed, insufficiently trained professionals; in operation, the law was used to stifle public knowledge of and disagreement with an unpopular traffic regulation technique.

A Government Is Not a Nation

Nations can exist just fine without secrets. Or they should be able to— it's hard to demonstrate this conclusively, because we don't have any control sample to use as a comparison. To put it another way, groups of people, large or small, can exist with or without a particular nation, and certainly without a particular government. Any group of people who have survived through a regime change demonstrates this.[2]

Using just one example from my own lifetime, the people of Hong Kong experienced an instantaneous change of their national status, with no immediate effect on the populace; one minute, Hong Kong belonged to England, the next minute, China. The people of Hong Kong did not instantly start eating a different type of food than they had the minute prior or go to new jobs or get new families. Their nationality had very little short-term effect on their lives. Typically, your nationality has almost no bearing on your day-to-day life. Now, your legal status (that is, how your government treats you) might change instantly, and those effects might develop in the years and decades to come . . . and people in Hong Kong are definitely going to be treated differently by their government today than they were prior to July 1997.

Government secrecy for purposes of "national security," then, is not required to preserve and protect a population; it is used to preserve and protect a government—a subset of the population that has power over the rest.

The argument to preserve governmental power typically invokes not the urge to protect a given population ("we need this government so our people do not die"), but instead the protection of a specific national "way of life" ("if our government changes, this will affect our entire way of life"). This is actually quite possible, judging by historical records; when some governments have fallen, the new governments have changed the daily lives of their citizens, sometimes very quickly, sometimes

---

[2] en.wikipedia.org/wiki/Handover_of_Hong_Kong accessed 05 APR 2020

dramatically, and sometimes fatally.[3] This is difficult to disprove or refute, because "way of life" is entirely subjective and ambiguous, and there is no metric or measure with which to judge any change. Effectively, it's a meaningless term; it cannot be defined or calculated. Like many such meaningless terms, it is most often used to evoke fear and suspicion to achieve political purpose ("vote for this referendum/person, or your whole way of life will change").

Rationales

Governments rarely talk about security and secrecy in the context of governmental self-preservation. Instead, there are a few "reasons" that governments use to justify secrecy. I will go through a few of them in this chapter and explain why the justifications are not rational, are not sufficient cause for the cost to implement them, or both. One particular "reason" used to vindicate government secrecy, however, was mentioned in the introduction and will be covered more thoroughly in Chapter 3—transactional privacy (where the government uses individual personal data during an exchange and therefore has an obligation to keep that's person's data protected). I will also discuss a few additional reasons why governmental secrecy is inimical to a society optimized for freedom.

Rationale: Direct Advantage

The first "reason" touted for government secrecy is usually advantage over other governments. If the government has some capability other governments do not, then the citizens of that government's country might enjoy some privilege (even if that privilege is only the sense of protection gained through superior might or lack of fear). For instance, nations with nuclear weapons typically expend efforts to ensure that nations without those weapons do not acquire them in the future.[4] Nuclear-capable countries have spent a great deal of time, effort, and money to prevent non-nuclear-capable countries from getting

---

[3] See the histories of El Salvador, Venezuela, and Cambodia.

[4] For example, the governments, intelligence agencies, and militaries of the United States and Israel supposedly operated in conjunction to release malicious software into the computer systems and engineering systems of an Iranian research facility to retard Iran's nuclear arms capability. www.zerodaysfilm.com

information and resources to create such weapons. Another aspect of this kind of secrecy is an advantage derived from having a particular informant or monitoring capability in another country, something that allows one government to learn about the actions of another (or about the actions/knowledge of people/organizations in another country).

In US military and government circles, this type of secrecy is referred to as *sources and means*; it consists of the way information is gathered from another country, which may have disclosed it, or the technology/ tools used to acquire and exfiltrate it. A source might be a person, such as a spy or a traitor in another country, or it might be a particular device or asset (such as a surveillance "bug" or a reconnaissance satellite), and means are the techniques and technologies used to deliver/acquire sources, intercept or interpret data, or perform an action that leads to an advantage or disadvantage.

Protecting a source is important to a government because it allows the government to continue using the source. If the adversary learns that a particular person is working as a source to exfiltrate information, the adversary might stop allowing that person access to sensitive information or use the person to deliver false information or possibly even kill that person. Secrecy allows the government to continually acquire information that it would not otherwise have access to.

Say a government has the capability to identify the location where an audio recording was made by the hum of nearby electrical components that are otherwise inaudible to the human ear.[5] If people (including another nation's government) were to learn of this capability, they might change microphone settings when recording audio so the hum is not captured, or they might edit the recorded audio to obscure/eliminate that sound. This would deny the government the capability to determine the location of the audio recording in that manner.

These reasons for secrecy make logical sense . . . if we all agree that it is the purpose of governments to continually acquire advantage over each other, either for themselves (the people in those governments) or for their citizens (the people served by those governments). If, however, we prefer a truly level playing field for competition and merit (be it for individual humans or for markets), this reasoning takes us into a

---

[5] A theoretical capability, anyway. www.schneier.com/blog/archives/2012/12/ detecting_edite.html and www.theregister.co.uk/2014/07/03/tinfoil_hatters_ spook_says_nsa_can_track_whistleblowers_through_power_lines

constant, ever-escalating competition with no possible end, affecting all areas of life. But, again—they make logical sense if it's the government's job to acquire and maintain advantage.

However, historically, this reasoning usually falls flat, because it fails so often in practice. Adversarial governments have motivation and great resources for acquiring each other's secrets and learning each other's sources and methods.

For instance, during the Cold War (in the late 20th century, after World War II, when the United States and the USSR [the Union of Soviet Socialist Republics, often referred to as the Soviets or Russia] were competing without engaging in open battle), the United States and the USSR expended massive amounts of resources to keep secrets from each other and to acquire each other's secrets. Two of the agencies the US government used to counter the USSR's ability to acquire US secrets were the Federal Bureau of Investigation (FBI) and the Central Intelligence Agency (CIA). This activity is generally called *counterespionage* by governments and consists of attempting to prevent other governments from learning your government's secrets. The FBI was tasked with counter-Soviet counterespionage activities within the United States, and the CIA was tasked with counter-Soviet counterespionage activities outside US borders.

Robert Hanssen[6] was an FBI agent who worked in various capacities over a 25-year span, including counter-Soviet counterespionage activities in both Washington, DC (at the FBI's J. Edgar Hoover headquarters building[7]), and New York City. For many years, he was also selling sensitive data to the USSR, including material that revealed some US human sources (spies) within Russia, some of whom were killed by the Soviet government. Similarly, Aldrich Ames[8] was a counter-Soviet counterintelligence officer for the CIA for 31 years, who also sold secret information to the USSR. The United States had similar assets and programs, including the Venona Project,[9] which used message intercepts

---

[6] Wikipedia. en.wikipedia.org/wiki/Robert_Hanssen#FBI_counterintelligence_unit,_further_espionage_activities_(1985%E2%80%931991)

[7] A complete aside: Some time after Hanssen's arrest, I worked as a contractor in the same room that the FBI had used to monitor Hanssen once they'd learned he was a Soviet mole.

[8] Wikipedia.en.wikipedia.org/wiki/Aldrich_Ames

[9] Wikipedia. en.wikipedia.org/wiki/Venona_project

(including a recording device placed, via submarine, on an undersea cable) to harvest Soviet secrets.

Between the two governments' efforts, a great number of the "secrets" they thought they'd kept from each other were known to the other. In fact, a significant amount of material that was protected from disclosure was known to the adversary for a considerable period of time. This is crucial to our understanding of secrecy (and privacy), because *both governments continued to expend a great deal of money and resources to "protect" those secrets, when the only people who were not aware of the information were the citizens of those countries.* That is, both governments knew the information. The only people who did not know the information were the people those governments purportedly served. The people who were supposed to decide how their government behaved, and which people would be allowed governmental privileges, were not allowed to properly monitor and review the actions of their governments and make informed decisions. And the resources that belonged to those citizens were taken and used by the government to "protect" information that was already known by the adversary.

Admittedly, this is a drastic oversimplification of how government (and particularly, military) secrecy works; just because a secret is known to some people in a government does not mean it is known to all people in that government (or that nation). Just because the CIA and KGB would steal secrets from each other's governments/organizations does not mean that the stolen secrets were always disseminated throughout the government/country that had stolen them. One of the common practices in secrecy is *compartmentalization*: promoting confidentiality by severely restricting access to a given set of assets to only those personnel who are deemed to have a direct *need to know*. Typically, this means that knowledge of the inner workings of any project is limited to only those personnel working on that project. So even when we're not discussing stolen material, not every secret known to someone who works in a government is known to all the people working in that government; secrets are often stovepiped such that the number of people who know them is purposefully minimal.

But this is not an adequate reason to justify secrecy as a practice or policy; in fact, it demonstrates another potential negative outcome: if secret programs and data are kept from wide distribution to increase confidentiality, there is a possibility of duplication of effort, as multiple organizations attempt to perform the same actions; because they are performing them in secret, each organization is not aware that the other organizations are doing the same things. This leads to a significant potential for waste, which is enormously troubling if these are government organizations, funded by tax revenue (private duplication of efforts, such as by competitors, minimizes resultant harm to only those investors of each company; government waste harms every taxpayer/citizen). There is almost certainly a person/office/committee that is supposed to oversee the various compartmentalized secret programs to avoid redundancy and waste, but this often does not scale well, for a variety of obvious reasons, especially in an ecosystem that naturally hides information. The United States, for example, has 330 million citizens, multiple military branches, 42 officially federally funded research labs,[10] and at least 16 agencies that are formally part of what is termed the "intelligence community"[11]; for any one entity to have coordinated, comprehensive oversight and understanding of the various components and operations of each is dubious.

Rationale: Overcome Other Secrecy

Also included in the concept of protecting sources and means is another justification for government secrecy: those sources and means used to pierce the secrecy of *other* governments must be confidential so that the target governments/organizations don't learn of them, defend against them, and keep their secrets. And the cost of those sources and means are also often kept secret as well, because even budgetary information might disclose some knowledge of what the sources and means are.

This rationale is also usually weak: often, information gathered through subterfuge or covert means is less valuable/valid than material acquired through what is called "open source" avenues—that is, data that is readily available to the public, either commercially or at no direct expense. There are uncountable private intelligence-gathering entities; some of these are often referred to as "news" agencies, or "the media." Spies and diplomats have used local news services and other open source entities for acquiring hard data for decades, if not centuries. Perhaps one

---

[10] Wikipedia. en.wikipedia.org/wiki/Federally_funded_research_and_development_centers
[11] Wikipedia. en.wikipedia.org/wiki/United_States_Intelligence_Community

of the best known open sources is Jane's Information Group,[12] which has published catalogs of the world's military vehicles for more than 120 years; Jane's books are often referred to by military and intelligence specialists as the definitive guide in such matters, even though the company is not sponsored by or a partner of any government.

There are many reasons for trusting open source information over data acquired through confidential means. First, with open sources, both the data and the source are immediately subject to verification and validation; if you know the source and means for data acquisition, you can estimate or account for biases in the collection. For instance, a confidential informant given a reward (monetary, or some other benefit) in exchange for "useful" information will have an incentive to generate or produce such information, regardless of the actual veracity of that data. Whether used in law enforcement or espionage (where informants are often referred to as HUMINT, for "human-sourced intelligence"), informants provide data for a variety of motivations, including financial reward, protection from being prosecuted themselves, revenge, personal thrill, and ideology. Any one of those motivations can also be cause for the informant to relay false or inaccurate information, particularly when the informant's identity and origin will remain protected. Likewise, the use of "jailhouse snitches" (that is, prisoners who produce information used to prosecute other prisoners) is infamous for the unreliability of the data produced in this manner, because the snitch is often incentivized through promises of a reduced sentence or favorable treatment and is already a known criminal (with a reduced level of trustworthiness to begin with).[13] Secrecy, then, increases the risk that the information acquired in this manner will be *less* valuable than material collected through open sources. Again, at the very minimum, the information gathered through open sources comes with the additional knowledge of the biases of the source.

And it's quite possible that the mechanisms used to keep sources and means of information-gathering confidential actually hinders the ability to act on or respond to information in a timely manner; the dissemination and sharing of that data with those personnel who can use it can be limited and hampered. An example: I was stationed in a military command center in Korea the day Kim Il-Sung died; we had

---

[12] Wikipedia en.wikipedia.org/wiki/Jane%27s_Information_Group
[13] www.innocenceproject.org/informing-injustice

access to multiple forms of classified communications channels, and the US government and military spent a substantial amount of money and effort to monitor North Korea extensively. Kim Il-Sung's death was an event of major military and political importance, as there was the potential for large-scale upheaval and a power struggle as the North Korea command structure dealt with the transition. There was also the possibility that the new regime would use the opportunity to enact plans to attack South Korea, a US ally, and we had to be ready to respond to any such attack according to our plans.

That day, the first notification to our command structure, the first mention we heard of the situation, did not come through any confidential or intelligence channels; it did not come from any sophisticated listening device or photo platform—we got a phone call from someone off-base who was watching the local South Korean television news, where rumors were spreading. Within minutes, we saw the same information being rebroadcast on CNN, via cable/satellite connection. It wasn't until sometime *after* these open sources had relayed the information that the command structure got verified confirmation from various classified sources.

Why? Information gathered through secret means requires protection and can only be released through a specific process and with proper formatting; preparing and transmitting a confidential message in government/military channels, and getting permission for the release of that message, takes a nontrivial amount of time. The information gathered through confidential sources and means might have the benefit of attribution, validation, and trustworthiness, but it takes time to disseminate, and that can delay action taken on that information, thus reducing the value of the data. The information gathered through the intelligence community could not keep up with the speed of the open source information, and in fact it was relatively quick and easy to verify the information provided by the open sources.

Is the expense of protecting data proportional to the amount of value lost in the speed of processing and production? That's hard to determine and often requires a significant amount of subjective analysis; classification of data is often tasked to the data owner—that person or office that is nominally closest to the collection and manipulation of the information.

That can lead to another problem with secrecy: perverse incentives of data owners to overclassify their assets, that is, adding more protections than are necessary to protect the value of the asset. Think of it as putting a \$10 lock on a \$5 bicycle; you are spending more to protect the asset than its replacement value, which is a waste of money. This can happen for many reasons and is the result of allowing human subjectivity into the process of assessing value. For instance, overclassification can be purely inadvertent—either accidental or because a particular data owner does not fully understand the classification scheme and misapplies a protection level (or fails to follow proper procedures[14]). This can often happen in organizations where not all personnel receive sufficient or uniform training on the classification and protection procedures. Or it can occur because the marking and handling procedures are too complicated.

There are other, less sympathetic reasons why a data owner might overclassify their assets. Classified material requires more protection, which entails a higher monetary budget for the office that "owns" the data—the manager of that office can increase the size and scope of their fiefdom, with more money and more personnel and more assets, than a manager of an office only engaged in unclassified processing. A manager might also be overclassifying out of a sense of personal fear; the manager understands that inadvertent disclosure of any data is blamed on the manager, so the manager might require additional, unjustified protections be placed on *all* data under the manager's control, to increase personal protection instead of appropriate and proportional protection of the data commensurate with the value of the assets. It might also be the result of a manager's laziness: an office where all data is classified at the highest level, and therefore requires a single, unified set of protections, is easier to manage than an office with assets at varied levels, which is more complicated and prone to accidental mislabeling/cross-pollination of data.

All of these very human outcomes are predictable when secrecy is implemented in a bureaucracy. Yes, proper oversight should limit the waste and problems associated with these practices . . . but human oversight is also fraught with human problems. (For example, the manager's

---

[14] A government official was questioned by the FBI about whether certain classified material was being protected according to proper procedures and regulations. The official claimed not to understand that a paragraph marked (c) in a government document meant that paragraph contained "confidential" material; instead, the official stated that the (c) would be cause for speculation . . . and suggested it may be a marking reflecting the order of the paragraphs in the document ["(a)," "(b)," "(c)," etc.].

manager is supposed to know if overclassification or misclassification is taking place, but that also adds costs to the process and is just as subjective and prone to human shortcomings.)

Conversely, efforts to remove information from compartments and speed its dissemination can also have adverse effects. The amount of data that Specialist Manning[15] and Edward Snowden[16] had access to was a direct result of an act of the US Congress following the 9/11 attacks, ordering the various American spy agencies to share classified data more efficiently. The amount of data each person could steal/disclose would be limited if each person was not allowed broad access to the material.

All of these problems associated with government secrecy might be accepted as normal risk resulting from good (or at least nonmalicious) human intentions; even the people who disclosed information counter to approved processes (Manning, Snowden) might be given the general benefit of doubt as wanting to act in accordance with moral ideals (although this may be arguable, and the detrimental effect might be viewed as outweighing whatever good was accomplished). However, secrecy also allows more inimical actions, also predictable when the power to hide information and act with privilege or impunity is granted to certain people.

For instance, in the United States in recent years, a number of widely publicized cases of police misconduct have come to light, with an almost alarming frequency. The fact that police have abused their powers is perhaps not so surprising; there is a tendency, when people are granted power over others, for the empowered to exercise that power, often in ways the unprivileged (often the people who granted those very powers) did not anticipate or intend. In regard to secrecy, the more salient (and somewhat terrifying) elements of these cases is how relevant and revelatory information was managed by the police, in a fashion that used secrecy on a level that could be perceived as calculated evil.

Here is the similar pattern of actions in these cases, almost uniform in their order and timing:

1. A victim accuses the police of an abuse (this could include a murder, an unjustified shooting, battery of the victim, or a wrongful arrest).

---

[15] Wikipedia. en.wikipedia.org/wiki/Chelsea_Manning
[16] Wikipedia. en.wikipedia.org/wiki/Edward_Snowden

2. The police officials/department issue a statement that the officers in question acted appropriately but that there is an investigation underway and that details will not be forthcoming until the completion of the investigation (that is, secrecy is necessary to keep the investigation as free from bias as possible, another justification often used when rationalizing governmental secrecy).

3. The police officials/department issues a statement that video of the abuse does not exist; it either is missing due to failure of recording equipment at the time of the abuse or was inadvertently deleted subsequent to the abuse.

4. Video of the abuse in question comes to light, either through an approved release from within the police department (a "leak") or from another, nonpolice source, such as a bystander with a camera/phone or a private surveillance camera.

5. Police officials are forced to recant and apologize, and finally some form of justice for the victim is offered (typically, some monetary compensation taken from taxpayer funds, with little to no consequence to the officers who engaged in the abuse or the officials who tried to minimize it or blame the victim).

Secrecy, then, in these cases (which, again, suggest a trend that is both predictable and awful) suggests the very possible potential for abuse of power, up to and including murder. I'll discuss the potential benefits of a nonsecret civilization throughout the book, but for the moment it is important to note that many of these recent abuses were only revealed—and the potential for justice to be meted appropriately—because of the ubiquity and easy availability of data that countered official statements from privileged and "trusted" authorities (dating back to the Rodney King case, where police officers were captured on video by a bystander with a private camera, beating King while he was on the ground and heavily outnumbered[17]).

One particularly egregious case took place in Baltimore in 2010; university student John McKenna was celebrating a sports team's victory in public, on the sidewalk of a city street. He was dancing and skipping, right until he realized he was standing in front of a unit of police officers mounted on horseback. McKenna froze—then one of the officers steered his horse into McKenna, slamming McKenna into a wall, and

---

[17] Wikipedia. en.wikipedia.org/wiki/Rodney_King

other officers moved in and clubbed McKenna on the ground.[18] While the attack was brutal and terrible, the subsequent actions by officers involved and their superiors elevated the activity to the level of evil: at least one of the police reports the officers filed claimed that McKenna, "struck those officers and struck their horses causing minor injuries."[19] The video later acquired by McKenna's lawyer show that the officers outright lied in their reports; McKenna did nothing to provoke the attack and does not appear to be engaged in any illegal activity whatsoever.

If the Baltimore police department had been able to maintain secrecy surrounding the situation and remained the sole arbiter of what the officers did during the attack, a grave horror would have gone without note. This can only happen with secrecy—it cannot occur when all information about every situation is known.

This is not to suggest that data transparency only protects unempowered people from those in the government; there has been more than one case where camera footage from the scene of alleged abuse has vindicated the actions of the police involved and cleared them of suspicion of wrongdoing. (One notable example is the case of Shaun King, who accused a Texas Highway Patrol Trooper of sexually assaulting and threatening her during a traffic stop; video footage from the officer's bodycam later proved these accusations false.[20])

It's painfully obvious that total openness of all information about all encounters greatly reduces the potential for false narratives.

Rationale: Military Advantage

Another reason used to justify governmental secrecy is particular to the military: secrecy is necessary to create an advantage over the enemy and to prevent the enemy from gaining an advantage over your own forces. This is a doctrine based on military history, using models some thousands of years old. Perhaps the best-known predicates of this military approach is Sun Tzu, who is presumed to have existed (the records are fuzzy) as early as half a century before the Common Era.[21] From Sun

---

[18] Please note: the video is extremely violent and disturbing. www.youtube.com/watch?v=uB91xjck5bY

[19] News media report on the abuse and the aftermath; again, the video is disturbing. youtu.be/rIS2XMwLE6c

[20] www.youtube.com/watch?v=apt17ot189o

[21] en.wikipedia.org/wiki/Sun_Tzu

Tzu's *The Art of War*: "Those who perceive beforehand the means of circuitous as direct are victorious—this is a fundamental in armed contention," which is a rather stilted way of saying, "if you know something your opponent doesn't, you'll win at war." Militaries adhere to these concepts today, prizing secrecy and maintaining a vast apparatus for controlling and protecting data.

First off: screw that. Just because something is old does not mean it's correct or useful; justifying a policy because it was used successfully by an ancient practitioner is worse than pointless—it's irrational and ridiculous. There are very, very few human endeavors that are the same now as they were 2,500 years ago; military activity is not some special exception.

This is *not* to say that we cannot glean useful practices/techniques from the past—there is nothing wrong with learning from previous mistakes or repeating something that was successful. It simply means that "because we've always done it this way" is no rational cause to maintain a particular practice.

Can a military campaign, battle, or action be successful in the absence of secrecy? I don't know—it's hard to find counterexamples, because secrecy is so steeped in military practice (and, I will concede, perhaps for good reason; not everything old is bad or wrong). But we do know this: political ends have been achieved without secrecy, even when those political movements *were directly opposed by overwhelming military forces.* Two examples that leap to mind are Mahatma Gandhi's[22] and Martin Luther King's[23] political protest actions (against the British Empire and the United States, respectively). Both those political campaigns can be successful even though they were waged in full view of the public and their opponents (indeed, without public view, those campaigns likely would not have succeeded). While it appears that I am conflating here both violent and nonviolent activities (warfare and protests), allow me some hubris to use old doctrine to refute old doctrine: Carl von Clausewitz[24] was a military philosopher who is also cited as creating the foundations for much of the modern approach to warfare; in his *On War*, Clausewitz underscores the point that military action is simply one type of activity on a spectrum of political activity, and war

---

[22] Wikipedia. en.wikipedia.org/wiki/Mahatma_Gandhi

[23] Wikipedia. en.wikipedia.org/wiki/Martin_Luther_King_Jr.

[24] Wikipedia. en.wikipedia.org/wiki/Carl_von_Clausewitz

is waged to achieve political goals. If this is true, then Gandhi and King both successfully defeated the armed forces they were against; this can be perceived as a military victory.

Please don't take this to mean I believe everyone should lay down weapons and therefore instantly defeat their armed enemies; I don't, and this would be foolhardy to an extreme degree. What I am saying is that there are strategies and tactics that can be deployed without secrecy and can still defeat a military opponent. There may be others that have not yet been explored and perhaps solely because our modern militaries subscribe to an outdated, ancient doctrine.

For example, secrecy in deployment of forces has long been maintained as paramount to the survivability of your forces; if the enemy doesn't know where your forces are, the enemy cannot strike and defeat/destroy your forces. Likewise, this secrecy offers the potential to surprise your enemy, perhaps giving your forces an advantage over opposing forces. However, it may be possible that this is not fundamental in all cases.

If the adversary knows your forces are approaching and what capabilities your military has, this does not necessarily mean the adversary can counter these capabilities. Instead, this may deny the adversary shelter/respite and cost the enemy resources; military superiority may simply exist through technological/training/logistics/economic advantage. If the enemy *knows* you will defeat them and there is no possible way for the enemy to succeed, the enemy may sue for peace or concede whatever it was you hoped to achieve through force. An example: when the United States used the atomic bomb on Hiroshima at the end of World War II, one of the stated intended outcomes was to bring about a definitive and timely end to the war with Japan, without the need to conquer the entire island chain of the country with ground forces (theoretically saving lives and material that would be lost in a prolonged conventional struggle). Prior to this use of the atomic bomb, its existence was kept secret; its public revelation was meant to convince the Japanese authorities to cease hostilities. (Arguably, the second use of an atomic weapon, at Nagasaki, was another demonstration to underscore this point; there is considerable historical argument whether this was necessary, or even if the first use was, but I'm not arguing that either way here.) This is a case where showing the enemy exactly what you are capable of was a means to defeat the enemy; bombing the city (and killing the people in it) did not somehow magically prevent the Japanese military from fielding troops or firing their weapons; all their munitions and forces were still operational. It did, however, put an end to their *political will to continue fighting*. This same argument was the basis of the US and Soviet doctrine of the Cold War, called *mutually assured destruction*, where each side knew the other's capabilities and that any war between them would not be survivable for either. Again, knowing the capability of each other's military forces, the *lack* of secrecy, created a situation where neither had the political will to engage in armed conflict. In fact, later discussions/agreements between the two powers would include provisions for allowing each to inspect the other's armaments to verify that each maintained similar capabilities.[25]

Moreover, military reliance on secrecy creates its own massive vulnerability, a vulnerability that will only grow as technology evolves. Technology development and ease of information capture and dissemination have created a situation where secrecy is becoming more and more difficult to achieve. When every 15-year-old has a device in their hand that can collect video, text, sound, location coordinates, and provide some level of veracity and validation, from anywhere in the world (and deliver to anywhere else in the world, quasi-instantly), hiding military activity/operations is a difficult proposition.

A startling demonstration of this was the landing of US special forces on a beach in Somalia, in 1992, as part of a military action called Operation Restore Hope.[26] While the activity was supposed to be secret, US troops were filmed and photographed as they arrived, by private news agencies that were waiting on the beach.[27]

Whether the presence of the reporters (or the broadcast of the information) affected the outcome of the operation is arguable, and not pertinent to the point: what was supposed to be secret was not, and the ubiquity of information capabilities only makes that possibility more likely in the future. If the success of the operation *had* relied on total secrecy, the operation would have failed. Therefore, any policy or doctrine requiring secrecy is going to become riskier, and the cost of trying to achieve secrecy will increase exponentially.

---

[25] Notably, the SALT and START agreements. history.state.gov/milestones/1969–1976/salt and www.state.gov/new-start
[26] Wikipedia. en.wikipedia.org/wiki/Unified_Task_Force
[27] CNN news feature, reposted to YouTube. www.youtube.com/watch?v=Xj9Fn3qG-Cw

In a world with no privacy, the military will have to adapt obsolete doctrine to achieve the same goals. It would be better to pave the way for that reality now rather than wait until military operations are shown to fail repeatedly. I have no solution for doing this; I am not a Sun Tzu or Clausewitz, and I severely lack the expertise and experience to even begin guessing at ways to create a new, viable approach to military operations. I can, however, foresee the issue and would hope this is being taken into account by those in a much better position to do so.

It is also worth mentioning that having a military that is successful only through secrecy may, in fact, be a net negative for a free nation . . . keeping military secrets from the populace runs into the same issues as other governmental secrecy and leads to military adventurism. Without true oversight (and approval, tacit or otherwise) of military operations by the people of the nation (either through their elected representatives or via referendum), the use of the military to deal with any and all political/diplomatic/human issues becomes both an easy answer and a tempting one for those in power. This might create an atmosphere that encourages imperialism (potentially a net negative for humanity, and for the home country/people of the military force) and groupthink bordering on brutality. To borrow an old adage, "when all you have is a hammer, everything looks like a nail." Reliance on the military for any and all purposes stifles innovation, lacks creativity, and devalues human life.

I want to be clear on that last point: the military is designed for two goals: killing people and breaking things. Modern militaries have become extremely proficient at achieving these ends; the military of my country (which I've served in, by choice, although I wasn't very good at it) is probably the most capable for this purpose that has ever existed. Because of this exceptional capability, Americans (both the populace and the politicians who serve them) tend to believe that any problem can be solved by judicious use of the military. There is a massive shortcoming to this tendency; the military solves problems through the use of force, which might not be the optimal solution for issues that do not pose a similar violent threat. Any use of the military necessarily creates risk for the troops being deployed (in my country, at the moment, these are citizens who volunteer for this form of employment and are some of the finest people I have known), as well as any people the military interacts with (foreign citizens, other militaries, etc.). Currently, this risk seems, to me, to be dismissed far too readily; putting our military members in harm's way seems to be viewed as the norm, for any or no appreciable, tangible benefit, as does the toll of human life and limb for any non-American. This is callous and crude and degrades what should be seen as most worth preserving: individual human lives.

This line of thought may be too philosophical and reveal my particular sensitivities. So, let me add this (more objective) point: using the military to address nonviolent concerns is simply not the option with the greatest utility. It is not a one-size-fits-all solution. To use an analogy, you can use a knife as a pry bar or a screwdriver or for other purposes, but that's not what a knife is for; a knife will be the most expensive and least effective pry bar you can possibly use.

Rationale: Hidden Diplomacy

One other justification for governmental secrecy is the facilitation of international diplomacy; the rationale goes like this: governments need to be able to negotiate in secret to come to terms that are beneficial to both. Typically, the excuse for this is to preserve the pride and political position of the politicians in the negotiation. For instance, if two countries are hostile, even if a politician in one country wants to make an overture to the other, the politicians in both countries might fear political repercussions, and therefore the countries will remain hostile. Those repercussions might, for instance, be electoral (that the electorate will view the politicians as "weak" for not wanting to continue hostilities), international (the government of a third country, when learning that the two hostile nations are negotiating, might be upset or frightened by possible results), or other reasons. Simply put, the belief is that secret negotiations must be secret for negotiations to exist at all, in many cases.

I find this total and complete nonsense.

If politicians do not have the strength of character, or strength of position, to represent the people of their constituency without needing to rely on deception (of either that constituency or other governments/nations), then those politicians have no legitimate reason for their position. A government, a nation, or even a treaty/agreement founded on lies lacks either sufficient merit or popularity and should therefore not exist.

Beyond my opinion, history bears this out: agreements made in secret do not magically result in better policies, for any country involved, other countries, or humanity overall. Secret negotiations allow *government security* to continue, without necessarily promoting *national security*, or security of the people or the species. This justification for governmental secrecy/privacy is weak and does not withstand any observation or test.

Rationale: Protecting Personal Privacy

The first has to do with the privacy of individual citizens; the government claims (somewhat correctly) that governmental transactions and pre-prosecution actions must be confidential in order to protect the identity/particulars of the people it interacts with or suspects of crime.

One example of this is monetary payments made by citizens. For instance, when you pay a fee for, say, a driver's license, via credit card, the government shouldn't reveal your credit card number, billing address, etc. This is not unique to governments; transactional privacy, often involving payment data, is a concern for every entity that exchanges money (including individuals). I will address that in Chapter 3.

Another example is when a law enforcement agency conducts an investigation prior to filing charges. If you are suspected of a crime, the government wants to keep your identity secret, for two main reasons: to not alert you of the investigation so that you do not destroy evidence or change behavior, making it harder to prosecute you, and also to not create an unfair, negative perception of you if you are inno-cent—sometimes, simply naming a suspect can cause distress to the sus-pect, including mob retaliation, reputational damage, etc.[28] Regardless, secrecy to conduct investigations should not be allowed simply because it's "easier" than other types of policing. The cost is often higher than the benefit.

Rationale: Emergency Powers

Another excuse for government secrecy, emergency powers, is rife with its own set of issues. All too often, a central authority will cite a given situation as transcending all others that have come before, some unique circumstance requiring unique excess of prior limitations on

---

[28] This is exactly what happened to Richard Jewell, the security guard who discov-ered the bomb set at the Olympic Games park in Atlanta and then was subsequently accused of setting it. The 2019 Clint Eastwood film on the subject is magnificent. www.richardjewellmovie.net

government. The justification goes, "yes, that was all well and good during normal times, but today is totally different *because* . . . ."

These rationalizations are often used for the most awful, misguided modifications to rule of law and many times result in pain much worse than whatever threat or danger they were meant to counter. This kind of ceding power to the government is usually requested in response to a "crisis" or exigent threat.

A particularly stark example of how government secrecy is used in this manner is from the American Civil War. During both the run-up to and the prosecution of the war, President Lincoln ordered the arrest of some 14,000 American and foreign civilians, including journalists, politicians, and people traveling between Union and Confederate states[29] . . . often without providing a reason why the arrest was effected or what the suspect was charged with (the writ of *habeus corpus*, or the charges leveled against a suspect, was first suspended by Lincoln and then confirmed by act of Congress later, both utterly ignoring the Constitution). Some of these political prisoners included former officers of the US military who came from Southern states, refused to take an oath of allegiance to the Union, and resigned their commissions at the outset of the war; they were immediately arrested and imprisoned.

Lincoln's justification for using such broad and severe measures was, of course, we're at war, and anyone who says anything against the government during wartime or protests government action or who refuses to swear to follow the government is an agent of the enemy. In fact, Lincoln specifically ordered that publishers who printed incorrect or false information be arrested and be tried by a military tribunal, ignoring Constitutional protections and rights altogether.[30]

Moreover, Lincoln was not shy about the use of force against political opponents or disregarding the freedom of Americans; he, himself, noted that he should have used *more* force against civilians: "... the time [is] not unlikely to come when I shall be blamed for having made too few arrests rather than too many."

When secret powers/programs are requested in this manner, for some kind of capability that supersedes all previous rules, it is almost always prefaced with caveats that this will be severely limited, that

---

[29] quod.lib.umich.edu/j/jala/2629860.0005.103/--lincoln-administration-and-arbitrary-arrests?rgn=main;view=fulltext

[30] www.presidency.ucsb.edu/documents/executive-order-arrest-and-imprisonment-irresponsible-newspaper-reporters-and-editors

it is absolutely necessary, and, often, that it will only be temporary. Whatever benefit this power provides, so the reasoning goes, cannot possibly be accomplished without requisite secrecy . . . and without said benefit, the very existence of humanity, the country, or your way of life is in jeopardy.

However, this justification falls flat for several reasons. First, it's almost always wrong: there is almost never a truly existential threat to all peoples or an entire country. Second, it is almost always regretted later, often because the harm it causes is proved to be greater (or equivalent) to whatever the impact of the perceived threat was. But, perhaps most importantly, any power that has ever been conferred on people with privilege, on the condition that this power would be constrained and minimized, has always been abused in a manner that exceeded the authority granted. Here, I cannot offer representative samples, because nothing would approximate the thoroughness of the truism: it is true in every case, so a list of historic cases is insufficient to make the point. I recommend you select any one you think may prove a counterargument and inspect it yourself, in the totality of human experience; you will find no exceptions.

Therefore, any special circumstances that give way to even the slightest bit of secrecy for one class, in contrast to all others, would crack the door of Pandora's box in a truly open society where there was no other secrecy.

No Net Benefit; Possible Net Negative

Most of this chapter has focused on responding to rationales used to justify governmental secrecy, but I'd like to finish with three additional important facets of the topic: reasons why government secrecy has no net benefit (and possibly a net negative) result.

Citizenry at Risk

First, an aspect tangentially mentioned earlier is that governmental secrets create a disadvantageous situation for the citizens of the country, where the government is allowed to keep information secret but the citizens are not. This creates a massive imbalance, and it's one that threatens the basic idea of a free nation. When the government hides information from the populace (or any part of the populace), the populace suffers. This is often rationalized as being done for "their own good" (where "their" is "the citizens") or as serving "the greater good" (where a number of citizens must sacrifice for the rest). This can be couched in any number of seemingly appealing ways, but it is extremely paternalistic and horrific when carried to its natural ends.

For example, the US Public Health Service spent four decades studying black men infected with syphilis (as well as other conditions, and a control group not similarly infected); during at least a portion of this time, demonstrably viable treatments for syphilis were commonly available and known to the doctors studying the patients but were withheld.[31] The justifications for this activity (or inactivity) were varied but were all flavors of the same theme: the data that can be accrued from this study will advance science, aid more people who suffer these conditions in the future, and the afflicted men are at least receiving more care than they would have if they had not participated in the experiment at all.

Today, of course, the obvious and egregious evil of this program, rife with medical ethics failings, racism, and lack of scientific candor and trust, is readily apparent. However, the underlying notions ("sometimes, the government must do things that are kept secret from the populace") still remain, creating a situation where the same atrocities could be perpetrated again, albeit in new forms. *Informed consent* is crucial here: it is unethical to treat someone (or not) for a condition *you* know they have but *they* do not, or to ask them to act (or not act) in a certain way, without their knowledge of the pertinent information. Consent is also the fundamental underpinning of government in a free country—the government should act only with the consent of the governed (a phrase I remember from somewhere). When the citizens do *not* have all the information about their government, and the government can act in secret, then the citizens are not consenting to the government's action. That violates the most elemental understanding of what a free nation should be.

A similar example, to stress the point, is the testing of atomic/ nuclear weapons in the United States in the mid-20th century. Over a period of years, the US government/military conducted more than 100 aboveground tests of atomic/nuclear weapons/devices; the explosions included radioactive debris/fallout. Both military personnel and

---

[31] Wikipedia. en.wikipedia.org/wiki/Tuskegee_syphilis_experiment

civilians were exposed to the effects of these blasts, some directly (at the test site) and some remotely (via fallout and particulate spread of the radioactive material, including tertiary exposure, such as drinking milk from animals that had been exposed); none of these people consented to the exposure (or, at the least, did not have informed consent, insofar as they did not understand the potential effects of the exposure).[32] Much of the information about these programs was considered secret and withheld from the populace (including those who were affected), to the point where many public claims of harm were disputed and denied by the government. This was done on the basis that these weapons were so important (and the information about the weapons' efficacy, as well as the results of the tests were so sensitive) to the "national defense" that sacrifices of individual people were negligible against the existential external threats of military opponents. The American people were not asked to make this choice of their own volition; that decision was made for them, by the policymakers who chose to make that value judgment on their behalf. While there are arguments that the citizens who elected those officials gave the officials a proxy to make such decisions on the citizens' behalf, this is weak and counter to the purpose. Unless the citizens are told, "now you will be choosing who gets to put a certain value on your life and may be making a decision to sacrifice you," the citizens are not acting with informed consent . . . and, even if that notification were to be part of our electoral process, the morality of such a "choice" is dubious—can a person be asked to hand another their own life, even by contract? In almost all other respects, this is considered illegal and immoral—I cannot hire someone to kill me, and in many jurisdictions I will be prevented by force if I attempt to do so. So, governmental secrecy creates the potential for immoral and inhumane activity.

Bad Public Policy

The second additional point, related somewhat to the first, is the real possibility of creating bad policy because of the pervasive use of secrecy. This will be explored in more depth in Chapter 5, but it's worth mentioning and describing here. If the government is allowed secrecy, then there is the real potential that one part of the government will create

---

[32] www.cancer.gov/about-cancer/causes-prevention/risk/radiation/i-131

public policy based on the *inaccurate information resulting from a secret program created by another part of the government.*

Gregory Treverton, in his book *Covert Action*, explains a fantastic example of just such an occurrence: in the 1980s, a civilian analyst named Claire Sterling had written about terrorist activity sponsored by the USSR; the CIA investigated the threat of global terrorism to lay the groundwork for programs to counter Soviet operations. However, CIA analysts who reviewed Sterling's sources eventually discovered that those sources were actually inaccurate propaganda created *by another division within the CIA.*[33]

The Secret Police State

The final additional point is the overall cost to any nation that allows governmental secrecy: the cost of secret agents and secret police. This is both a financial cost (the expense of maintaining a massive force of covert assets used to both investigate the secrets of other countries, and to protect its own country's secrets) and a social/moral cost. The former is simple to understand. The second is a bit more insidious.

Each concession a nation makes to secret policing brings it a little closer to a nation that is not free. Typically, governments claim the need for secret police in order to counter criminals; open policing is more difficult and decreases an advantage for law enforcement. In traffic enforcement, for instance, drivers will often slow down when they see a police cruiser, but an unmarked police car will be able to catch speeders. This is a perfect example of the problem: is the purpose of police to make society safer or to apprehend and prosecute lawbreakers? The marked police car slows down traffic . . . ostensibly making drivers safer, which is the purpose of the speed limits. The unmarked car allows speeders to be caught and fined. This type of policing, again, causes perverse incentives for the law enforcers and the government, as the fines for law violation become a source of revenue for the government. It may also cause an adversarial perspective for police and the populace; the police view the citizens as potential lawbreakers who should be "gotten," and the citizens view their police as nannies and scolds (or worse) who should be avoided and distrusted.

---

[33] Gregory F. Treverton, *Covert Action: The Limits of Intervention in the Postwar World*, I.B. Tauris & Co Ltd (January 1, 1988) pg. 165

Another aspect of secret policing that degrades the social contract in a free nation is lack of oversight. I mentioned this earlier in the chapter, but it's important to reinforce that idea. When a law enforcement body is allowed to operate in secret, keeping not only the sources and means of evidence collection covert but also the results of these efforts, it is impossible for the citizens to gauge the efficacy and efficiency of these programs and to make informed consensual choices regarding the cost/benefit trade-offs. This is especially dangerous when the cost is freedom and the benefit is intangible or immeasurable.

For example, the National Security Agency (NSA) instituted a program after the 9/11 attacks that allowed the agency to collect information about the telecommunications activity of Americans at large, without the need for establishing probable cause of criminality or first obtaining a court order (warrant/subpoena).[34] More than once, NSA officials lied to their own government about the existence of this program, or any effort to accomplish these ends.[35] The existence and full extent of the program was revealed to the public by Edward Snowden in 2013, as part of the information he illegally obtained and published.[36] The NSA defended the program, claiming it had successfully prevented at least 50 terror attacks, including some aimed at US targets.[37] However, other government sources publicly stated skepticism of these claims.[38] Then just six years after Snowden's revelations, the NSA called for discontinuing the program, claiming that it was not effective in counter-terror efforts.[39]

The citizens are left to wonder and make supposition, with no effective way to understand the risks and potential benefits of this program, to determine whether elected and appointed officials responsible for protecting Americans (both against terror attacks and governmental overreach) acted in the best interests of the citizens, whether these programs

---

[34] Wikipedia. en.wikipedia.org/wiki/PRISM_(surveillance_program)

[35] sensenbrenner.house.gov/2018/3/james-clapper-not-charged-with-lying-to-congress [Full disclosure, Representative Sensenbrenner appointed me to the Air Force Academy at the outset of my academic and military careers.]

[36] www.cnet.com/news/some-companies-helped-the-nsa-but-which

[37] abcnews.go.com/Politics/nsa-director-50-potential-terrorist-attacks-thwarted-controversial/story?id=19428148

[38] www.nbcnews.com/news/world/nsa-program-stopped-no-terror-attacks-says-white-house-panel-flna2D11783588

[39] eandt.theiet.org/content/articles/2019/04/nsa-recommends-end-to-controversial-mass-surveillance-program

(or similar programs) produce any viable results, and whether their own money (given to the government) was spent in accordance with their best interests or even in a responsible manner. Without insight, there is no possible way to provide informed consent, and no way to know how to correct the situation. Furthermore, it erodes public confidence in their own representatives and officials, and the entire notion of rule of law, as well as trust and basic fairness. If I lie to a lawmaking body or law enforcement agent, I can go to prison; a government official doing the same thing gets a promotion.

The use of secret sources and means and an extensive secret police apparatus additionally harm the social fabric in one other vital aspect: these secret enforcement programs often use anonymous reporting to maximize information gathering, often allowing one citizen to report the suspected wrongdoing of another. This degrades the trust not only between a populace and its government but between individual citizens; it breeds mistrust of everyone and everything, every relationship and interaction. For example, records suggest that while East Germany was a totalitarian member state of the USSR, one out of every 30 citizens was reporting on other citizens . . . and that the secret police kept files on up to 33 percent of its own citizens.[40] With that volume of secret police activity, it is impossible to imagine any kind of human interaction untainted by distrust and apprehension. The impact to quality of human life is incalculable.

People will often trade freedom for security; it is perhaps one of the oldest human cost/benefit analyses. And there is veracity to the claim that it will be more difficult for law enforcement agencies to effectively perform their tasks without the use of secrecy. I regret that I cannot remember who said it, or the quote in verbatim, but there is a simple counter to this prospect: it is not supposed to be easy for law enforcers to do their job; when it is easy for law enforcement to act, we end up with a police state.

---

[40] fee.org/articles/10-terrifying-facts-about-the-east-german-secret-police

3

Privacy and Personal Protection

And I don't feel safe anymore, oh what a mess.
I wonder who's watching me now. Who? The IRS?!
— *Kennedy "Rockwell" Gordy*

The justifications for institutional privacy, as discussed in Chapters 1 and 2, are largely disingenuous, for the reasons discussed there. But most individuals are more concerned with their own personal privacy than secrecy granted to organizations (although people are often anxious that their privacy is being harvested and used by institutions as opposed to other individuals). When surveyed specifically on the subject, people consistently respond that they have no control over their own data and that they are concerned with losing personal privacy.[1]

What is it that people worry about, in terms of losing privacy, and are those fears viable?

One of the most obvious individual concerns related to privacy is financial protection; if you know my credit card number, my PIN, my login data, my bank account number, the combination to my bike lock, the times I'm not at home, and where I keep the key to my safe deposit box, you can take all my money and all my possessions.

Theft is probably chief among the perceived threats to personal security; someone taking what is yours is a direct individual harm (and, beyond the obvious financial loss, the immeasurable harm of the sensation of violation and exploitation is very real, if not tangible). Many people consider privacy essential for preventing theft. Moreover, privacy

---

[1] www.pewresearch.org/internet/2019/11/15/americans-and-privacy-concerned-confused-and-feeling-lack-of-control-over-their-personal-information

or secrecy regarding financial transactions is also expected by and for the institutions we engage with—the companies we purchase goods and services from, and the government agencies that we have to pay (as mentioned in Chapter 2, regarding justification for transactional data secrecy); if the database of the store where I use my debit card is breached, I could still lose money from my account, even though I protected my data sufficiently, and it was the store's security that failed.

Throughout this chapter, I'll go through a range of specific fears, in turn, and consider their dependence on privacy as the sole (or primary) means of security.

Your Exposure

Is financial theft an actual threat? It depends on your jurisdiction, the financial medium you use, and how valuable your time is. In the United States, for instance, individual customers are not legally or financially responsible for fraudulent payment card transactions (beyond a certain statutory minimum amount, which is usually waived, anyway).[2] Instead, the liability falls on either the issuing institution (the bank/credit agency) or the merchant that processed the transaction. When banks tell customers about all the important and impressive security features involved in your financial protection, these are somewhat misleading; these measures are not to protect you, the customer—they are to protect the *bank*. So, from an individual perspective, this is a misbegotten fear, for the most part: individual loss associated with payment card fraud is almost negligible.

There are caveats to that *almost*, though.

■ You may need to demonstrate that you did not make the fraudulent transaction and prove you weren't the one making the purchase (or the beneficiary). This can take considerable time and effort, which does entail some personal expense. You might not have immediate access to the funds in question until the investigation is resolved, which can have a truly deleterious impact.

[2] US Code, Title 12, "Special Credit Card Provisions," www.law.cornell.edu/cfr/text/12/1026.12

- Certain types of unauthorized purchases might not be your legal responsibility, but you may end up financially damaged nonetheless. For instance, the child of a cardholder might make the purchase without the parent's knowledge; the parent might choose to accept the financial responsibility instead of having the child charged with a crime. Ditto for spouse, sibling, friend, whoever. The law does not protect from that sort of exposure.

And this protection only extends to payment card transactions; other financial instruments, particularly those that are tangible (money, precious metals, etc.) are not protected in this manner . . . perhaps ironically, because of the relative secrecy (through anonymity) of their nature of exchange.

Expounding on this, cash doesn't create a record, a log, when you spend it; unless extra effort is taken (creating a bill of sale, a receipt, etc.), cash can change hands with no trace. This makes it optimum for privacy, through anonymity—if you want to buy something and you want no history of the exchange, you use cash. However, this also makes it ideal for thieves: when someone unauthorized takes your money, it's relatively difficult to demonstrate that the money was yours (sans extraordinary circumstances, like recording the serial numbers on the bills themselves while they're in your possession; and even then, the stolen bills would need to be found in the possession of the thieves—if they were already spent, you'd have no ability to prove that you weren't the person who spent them). Conversely, the very public nature of the payment card (a concrete record on both sides of the transaction) is what makes it resistant to fraud (or at least readily detectable and rife with evidence).

And here is a departure from the idea of confidentiality as the sole means of personal protection; this is quite similar to the discussion of institutional trust in Chapter 1 and how secrecy and privacy are not always the best means to achieve the desired goal (getting the best personnel for each position of trust/privilege). Confidentiality (that is, secrecy) is one way to attempt to secure a transaction, and we use many types of controls to provide confidentiality, including encryption, access management, and physical locks (among many, many others). However, another way to accomplish this same goal (and often combined with confidentiality controls) is through full and open attribution, that is, a total lack of secrecy.

Check Yourself

One aspect of open attribution is nonrepudiation: none of the parties to the transaction can deny having taken part in the transaction. This is what protects the cardholder from the fraudulent credit card purchase; the record of the purchase itself helps prove the fraud (or lack thereof).

To make the case, until fairly recently in banking history, a significant portion of consumer purchases were not made with electronic payment cards; they were made with personal checks. A check is a formal, written, public record of the transaction: the check lists who made the payment, who received it, the date of the transaction, the account information where the payment is drawn from, and the authenticating element (the customer's signature). None of these things are hidden; anyone looking at the check can readily see all the elements of the transaction (although, in the later years of paper checks, there were many nonobvious security elements that were embedded in the check itself). This was not a private transaction, in any regard, yet it was still widely perceived as relatively safe (at least compared to cash) and secure.

I am not suggesting we go back to writing checks to avoid the pitfalls of privacy/secrecy, in the same way I'm not advocating we use cash for everything to gain anonymity. Both those instruments are physical and therefore considered cumbersome and slow compared to digital transactions today. However, the same principles we might find appealing in the use of the credit card (viewable register of the transaction) and cash (rudimentary anonymity) might be accomplished through other, more modern means.

For instance, the same concept used to make personal checking viable (open attribution) can be found in today's implementation of cryptocurrency. Cryptocurrency, perhaps best known to most people in the form of Bitcoin, uses an open, public register of transactions to ensure trust and value of the medium. In fact, that is all cryptocurrency is: a finite set of numbers (the electronic coinage), assigned to specific accounts (the owners of the various amounts), and a log of all the exchanges of those numbers. Any transaction must be registered in the public ledger for the "coins" to be exchanged. This might offer the protection of attribution (everyone, everywhere, can watch the transactions, in quasi-real time, of everyone else, and thus we know who is the rightful owner of each "coin"), as well as the anonymity of cash (your account number is not exactly you, in terms of your identity, and therefore even the people

watching transactions do not know just who is who, or what they purchase with their "coins").

Cryptocurrency is not a magical solution, and I'm not suggesting it's
the ultimate protection against theft; I only use it here as an example of
an approach that is not wholly reliant on confidentiality to secure transactions. And it's essential to point out that cryptocurrency has many of
the same failings as the older value instruments: it does require *some*
secrecy if you want true anonymity and security—you can't publish
the secret encryption key you use to register the transaction, or anyone
could access your electronic "coins" and send your money to themselves,
and you must keep your key or get locked out of your own money, etc.
But this is a useful counterexample for why we are not wholly reliant
on privacy/secrecy to secure our transactions.

To carry this notion a step further, if your bank can view you, through
any and all monitoring capability (video, audio, online, etc.) both historically and in real time, it would be quite easy to determine whether
you conducted a transaction or whether someone else did. Refuting a
fraudulent charge would be straightforward; the bank audit/security
team would only have to review your actions at the time of the transaction to determine whether you participated. There would be no deni-
ability and no need for further substantiation. Moreover, there would
be a corresponding record of who actually did execute the transaction,
evidence of their own crime.

Another reason why an individual might want personal privacy
is the threat of blackmail; an attacker will reveal something about
you to someone else (your spouse, your family, your employer, your
government, etc.) if you do not comply with the attacker's request
(usually, for money). As explained in Chapter 1, this kind of threat is
diminished when institutional trust is not wholly reliant on secrecy and
aspects of personal/individual privacy. In Chapter 7, I will explain why
a post-privacy world will largely be free of blackmail risk altogether.

Personal privacy might also be seen as a bulwark for personal trust,
which is used in modern economies to establish and maintain a credit
rating. A credit rating is just an economic measure of trust, as declared
by a third party (not a vendor or customer, but a credit bureau). Theoretically, without privacy (or really, security), someone could pretend to
be you, run up bills in your name, not make payments, and negatively
affect your credit rating; this can impact your ability to acquire financial
credit or cause any financial services (loans, extended transactions, etc.)

to be more expensive for you (higher interest rates, higher transactional costs, etc.).

Again, this issue can be addressed through the use of nonrepudiation, instead of privacy. A truly open record of your activity would demonstrate which purchases you've made and which you haven't. Personal financial trust could be pegged to your actual activity, as opposed to identifiers that represent you (credit card numbers, bank account numbers, tax ID numbers, etc.). This is not much different than the explanation of why privacy is not necessary to protect against theft.

Take Your Medicine

Another potential need for privacy is medical information and how it may affect an individual's potential for benefits (where "benefits" may be life/health insurance, romantic partners, employment advantage, and so forth).

Examples include:

- An underwriter determines that you are in a high-risk category (you have developed a new medical condition/disease or you have started racing motorcycles as a hobby or you have taken up smoking); the underwriter may choose to increase the price of your term life insurance policy or not renew it at all.
- All the potential romantic partners in your community become aware that you have (or have had) a sexually transmitted infection and decline your advances.
- A potential employer has to choose between hiring you and other suitable candidates; the employer learns that you have a chronic condition that disallows you to perform the required work 20 percent of the time, while competing candidates do not.

Medical data can be determined from a number of sources: your family history, DNA markers, your actual medical files, and so forth. Medical conditions might also be gleaned or interpreted from your history of financial transactions: if you use your credit card to pay for a visit to an oncology clinic, someone viewing your credit history might suppose you have cancer or are concerned about developing cancer.

Some of these data sources can be protected through the use of anonymization, as opposed to other privacy measures (stripping out identifiers, as opposed to trying to keep information secret). However, this can also convey additional risks: medical information that is in your best interest to share with various providers (specialists, hospitals, pharmacists, etc.) might not be associated with *you*, because your identity has not been sufficiently bound with your medical records; this can cause a failure of your medical providers to give you proper treatment.

The same societal problems that stem from institutional privacy may also be associated with medical privacy: greater expense than the potential loss due to risks, disproportionate advantage for those entities that have access to secret information, risk of corruption/blackmail/impropriety, etc.

It's difficult to predict how a post-privacy world might address these problems/needs. Some medical aspects of life might be improved, while others might decline. Although speculative, here are some possible benefits:

- If you are aware of the sexually transmitted infections in all the potential romantic partners in your community, you can make more informed choices about your own romantic involvements. This makes it far easier to avoid HIV, hepatitis, and similar costly health risks.
- If everyone's medical data is widely known, it becomes easier for researchers to aggregate and disaggregate data. This can lead to new treatments and more effective public awareness campaigns, which everyone could ultimately benefit from.[3]
- Similarly, it becomes easier for you to identify in advance whether you are at higher risk for a particular problem and take preventative action before the problem ever develops.
- It is also conceivable that once everyone's medical histories are completely known, you might not suffer punitive damages for your medical conditions. Insurance companies, healthcare providers, and hospitals are all businesses that need to make a profit. Almost everyone in society has medical situations to deal with across the course of their lives. Insurance and healthcare

---

[3] For instance, during a 2019 interview, Anne Wojcicki, founder and CEO of 23andMe, a DNA testing company, made it clear that the cost of personal testing kits was intended to be offset by pharmaceutical research firms seeking larger data sets in order to create more effective treatments. freakonomics.com/podcast/23andme

companies might be able to maximize their profit best by distributing costs across the entire populace, balancing out prices based on long-term projections of how much people can pay for things and when. It has the potential to transform entire industries to the benefit of each person.[4]

Obviously, some of these ideas are more speculative than others, and they are just the tip of the iceberg. Ditching medical privacy may or may not convey these or other societal benefits. A great deal of analysis still needs to be done to explore the various variables.

The Scene of the Crime

Another obvious goal of personal privacy is physical protection; if someone hostile knows where you are, they can reach you in order to harm you. However, uniform lack of privacy for all parties diminishes this risk: if you know where *they* are at all times, you know if they are in a proximity to cause you harm. You can either escape, defend yourself, or call upon aid at the specific time and location necessary.

This is preferable to the current situation, for instance, in the United States; all too often protection (in the form of police/law enforcement) is not available in a timely manner, and aid is only rendered after harm has been committed.[5]

Moreover, total knowledge of identity, location, and time may act as a deterrent factor for those intent on committing physical violence in any mindset short of complete detachment from reality: if I know that I will be placed, irrefutably, at the scene of a crime and that my actions will be known subsequent to whatever transpires, I may be less inclined to commit that crime or cause that violence.

Again, this may not abrogate the possibility of those crimes that are wholly irrational—crimes of passion, domestic violence, psychopathy, and so forth. However, the targeted victims of these crimes will be in a much better position to protect themselves than they are currently.

---

[4] For an excellent introduction to actuarial math used by insurers, I recommend Sal Khan's fantastic video on the topic, www.khanacademy.org/economics-finance-domain/core-finance/investment-vehicles-tutorial/life-insurance/v/term-life-insurance-and-death-probability
[5] onlinelibrary.wiley.com/doi/abs/10.1002/casr.30477

TOTALLY TRANSPARENT PROTECTION

Using the premise described in the Introduction, how would total transparency offer personal protection from physical threats?

Let's start with the perceived risk—the thing we worry about when we imagine total loss of privacy. We believe that if anyone can view us at any time, a person with dangerous motivation (be it grudge or attraction) can observe us, find us, and hurt us. We're especially afraid of strangers stalking us and surprising us in order to harm us.[6]

Right now, that fear is enhanced by our pseudo-privacy: people we don't know can view our social media feeds, our credit records, data from our personal devices, and so forth. People who have hostile intent can learn about our behavior, observe us, and ultimately find us. We have no way of knowing who is watching us and who might intend to do us harm.

But without privacy, we would have access to all data, *including data about who is watching us.*

Envision this: you have access to all data feeds, everywhere, all the time. Of course, you can't possibly ingest all that data—you simply do not have the time to watch everyone else on the planet constantly, trying to determine who wants to harm you, personally. Heck, you don't even have the time to watch *one* other person in real time; one second of their existence is one second of yours, so your entire life would be spent viewing that person. But what if you harnessed computing power and mathematical capability along with your access to data?

Say there was an app (or 10 or 20) that "watched" data feeds for you and tracked every instance when someone was watching you. Every time someone says your name within reach of a microphone (any microphone, including a phone belonging to someone else standing nearby, but not party to, the conversation) or every time someone views your social media page(s) or every time someone drives by your home or through your neighborhood . . . the app notices and makes a record of that specific person paying attention to you.

The app has a threshold; how much "attention" is normal, and how much is worth worrying about? People who pay more attention to you

---

[6] We believe this, and fear violence from strangers, even though it's just as likely that someone we know (often, someone we live with) is more likely to commit a violent crime against us, www.bjs.gov/content/pub/pdf/cv18.pdf

than is normal are flagged for additional observation, and the app watches their behavior in more detail. Is this person collecting data about you? Saving photos of you? Saying things about you that might be threatening? Engaging in behavior that might be inimical toward you? You might modify the threshold for specific people you know mean to do you harm—someone you have harmed in the past, someone who has threatened you, a jaded former spouse/partner, etc. The app tracks those people more carefully. If you're a public figure (you have some celebrity status or are an elected official, etc.), the threshold set on your app might be different than someone else's app—your name is going to come up in conversation more often than other names.

If someone watching you seems to rise to the level of a tangible threat, you can determine how you want to address the situation. Is the person near your location? Are they moving toward your location? With access to all data feeds, you can know as much about them as they know about you—you can track their location, in real time, the same way you can watch a pizza delivery vehicle on a map on your phone. Even if the "attacker" isn't carrying their own electronic device or broadcasting their location, even if they are trying to hide from observation, you can still observe their movements and activity: you have access to every other data feed. You can view the video from every camera, whether it's on a traffic pole, attached to a cash machine, or every view-enabled doorbell in your neighborhood (or the attacker's neighborhood). You can monitor every purchase the attacker makes, including whether they purchase a plane ticket to travel to the city you live in. You can use facial recognition (and other monitoring technologies) to locate the attacker and maintain full and current knowledge of their whereabouts.

When do you want to react to the potential attacker? It's up to you. You can determine when they've gotten too close for your comfort. How do you want to respond? That's also completely up to you: you have the data, and you determine what risk is acceptable. Do you want to lock yourself in a secure room whenever they are nearby? Do you want to call a friend to come over and wait with you? Do you want to hire a team of security guards to protect you? Do you want to call the police? Ask a judge for a restraining order? Do you want to move away from where the attacker is (and where the attacker is going), putting more distance between you and them? Do you want to go to a public place, where the presence of more people might be reassuring? Do you want to buy a gun?

Today, with "privacy," you can be surprised by an attacker, completely unaware even that this person wanted to do you harm. In a post-private world, you never have to be in the same location as the attacker; you can always be one step ahead, never surprised. You know who is watching you, and you can create a reasonably accurate estimation of just who intends to do you harm. For physical harm to take place, you and the attacker typically have to be in the same location; with total transparency, that never has to occur.

You're a Celebrity

Finally, personal privacy might be seen as a protection from intrusive/invasive types of behaviors that might be seen as negative yet short of physical harm. This could include harassment, emotional harm, threats, and the like. In recent years, with the evolution of digital communications, we've seen examples where an otherwise unremarkable person has been elevated to heights of infamy almost instantly and become a target for public revilement and hostility.[7] This might be construed as particularly terrifying when we consider that anyone famous, throughout human history, has often been targeted by violent maniacs *whether the famous person was adored or loathed*.[8] In the digital age, when any one of us might become famous (or infamous) for something we might do (or even be accused of doing), the potential for attracting crazed individuals who intend us harm exists for all of us. Sacrificing privacy means exposure to that kind of deranged hostility.

However, lack of privacy is both sword and shield; while it is possible that the previous protection of blending in with the ordinary crowd of

[7] Entertaining journalist Jon Ronson has written an entire book about the phenomenon, including some fascinating case studies. Ronson, J. (2016). *So you've been publicly shamed*. London: Picador.

[8] Politicians, entertainers, sports figures, the wealthy, and anyone else who might be considered largely admired by the public is often just as likely to attract violent-minded adherents as criminals, villains, and those demonized by the public. People have harmed or tried to harm US President Gerald Ford (twice), Beatles John Lennon and George Harrison, Pope John Paul II, cannibal serial killer Jeffrey Dahmer, and assassin Lee Harvey Oswald. Celebrity entails risk.

the population may have isolated most people from the threats/risks that celebrity status would confer, those risks/threats that might emerge as a single person (any person, in a nonprivate world) becomes noticed by others are also somewhat mitigated when privacy is removed from the equation.

Much like the prior example of direct physical harm is ameliorated by the full knowledge of the location and intent of potential attackers, the impact and potential for online information-based attacks are diminished when privacy no longer exists, because no online attacker can act anonymously. If we all know the source and identity of every person sending/posting harassing material, then it is less likely that people will be inclined to harass others, and we will all be able to deal with them appropriately if they do. We will also be better prepared to sort the ones with true violent intent from those who are simply trolling for attention or jumping on a grievance bandwagon. And for those who simply continue to spew negative content, it will be easier to create communication filters for recipients.

NOTE   It's virtually impossible to identify solutions for every concern that may result from a post-privacy world, but I can predict a new product/service that might evolve in this situation: a Known Trolls filter list for people who cannot resist the temptation to lash out at others; because their actions and identities will be known, preblocking them could be a matter of subscribing to a simple update.

4

A Case Against Privacy: An End to Shame

"It's called a confidence game. Why? Because you give me your confidence? No. Because I give you mine."
—David Mamet, House of Games[1]

Aside from security protections, you only need privacy for things you are ashamed of.

Shame has two general flavors.

- Being ashamed of who you are/what you do, yourself, because of how it makes you feel
- Being ashamed of who you are/what you do, because of how others will treat you

I'll call these two versions of shame *self-shame* and *context-shame*. A person can feel both types of shame about a single behavior, or one or the other.

Self-shame generally requires a larger context; it cannot be produced in the absence of other people or the larger fabric of a social construct. A person who had never experienced interaction with other people would simply do whatever was necessary to bring satisfaction or pleasure and to avoid pain. They would have no reason to act otherwise. A person must learn that a natural behavior is unappealing to other humans in order for the person to feel shame about that behavior.

As with self-shame, context-shame exists due to the dynamic of a larger social interaction. This isn't a uniquely human trait, either. It is shared with any animal that has enough capacity to learn rules. Anyone

---

[1] Hausman, M. & Mamet, D. (1987) House of Games. United States. Filmhaus

who has ever had a pet dog has seen this type of reaction: the dog will gladly do something it knows to be against your rules, because that is the dog's nature. However, once the dog realizes you, the owner, have detected the unruly behavior, the dog will behave in a much different fashion, demonstrating contrition or fear of punishment.

I had a dog that loved to roll on any animal carcass it found in the woods and was eager to do so, acting gleeful (wagging its tail, moving in a frisky manner, etc.). However, when I would encounter the dog after it had rolled on a carcass, the dog would drop its head and tail and move slowly, carefully treading with each paw away from me. (It's important to note that while I had remonstrated the dog verbally for rolling on carcasses, I never struck the dog or physically corrected it in a way that would justify a fear of abuse, so the dog's reaction to detection was a demonstration that the dog understood it had violated my rules and was aware of those rules, but this was not sufficient for the dog to check similar future behavior.)

Generally, the behaviors linked with shame are often bodily functions, sex, ingestion, elimination, etc. These almost always bring relief or joy and would not be shameful unless we were taught to feel shame for them.

For example, emptying your bladder brings relief from the discomfort of having a full bladder. A baby does not need to be taught to relieve its bladder; it can do this naturally. However, the results are messy and can be unhygienic and cause other discomfort (rash, irritation, etc.). So, we train children to use a toilet and have them drain their bladder there. This becomes a mark of minimal human capacity in a civilized society; anyone who relieves their bladder while still fully clothed might feel ashamed or embarrassed by their lack of bodily control. Lack of bladder control might happen for any number of reasons; physical infirmity, inebriation, fear response—these are all understandable and widely known. However, for the person who is lacking control, incontinence is *still* a source of shame, because it demonstrates an incapacity, making the individual feel somewhat "less" than others.

So, for a lack of bladder control, the person might feel self-shame ("I am less than almost all other adults") as well as context-shame ("other people will mock me and laugh at me"). Privacy, in this type of situation, protects the person with the bladder control problem, but only from the context-shame. Even if the person finds a secretive solution to their situation (say, adult diapers that trap moisture and smell and are not noticeable under clothing), this does not address any self-shame the person might feel about their abilities relative to those of other adults.

Personal privacy, in this example, might serve another purpose, beyond avoiding shame; if the loss of bladder control is perceived as an element in an overall pattern of diminishing abilities, the person suffering from this condition may want to mask that element to avoid detection of the pattern. For instance, an elderly person may be afraid that they will lose personal autonomy if their adult children learn that the parent's physical capabilities are degrading. Perhaps the adult child is considering taking away an automobile the parent is allowed to use or is considering putting the elderly parent in a nursing home with continual medical monitoring. If the elderly parent's bladder condition becomes known to the adult child and the adult child is tracking the overall health of the elderly parent (diminished eyesight, memory problems, etc.), then the adult child may be more likely to reduce the elderly parent's freedoms and privileges. So, the elderly parent hides the condition from the adult child; privacy avoids the loss of choices.

Is privacy good and preferred in situations like these? I am not so sure. To me, it seems that loss of privacy, a world of total knowledge, would improve these situations and would remove the potential for secondary and tertiary negative effects that stem from the use of privacy. It seems likely that an end to privacy would lead, eventually, to an end to many potential sources of shame.

If an individual understands the true overall context of their condition, the individual may suffer less. If the adult with the bladder control problem realizes there are many other capable adults who also suffer from bladder infirmities, the individual may not be as ashamed. Would the elderly person then be less inclined to feel shame at the loss of bladder control? And, perhaps, would the elderly person be more inclined to make the problem known, and seek medical attention, if the outcome did not include shame?

Moreover, if *others* are aware of the individual's condition, and the source of it, the possibility that adults would context-shame the individual are decreased. For example, if the adult children of the elderly person had total knowledge of the elderly parent's infirmities and situation (the loss of bladder control, combined with any other medical conditions), would this lead to less freedom of choices for the elderly parent, or more? If the loss of bladder control is not indicative of a totality of capabilities that entails greater risk for the elderly parent and anyone else around that person, then knowledge of that condition would not necessarily lead to any imposition on the parent's liberties. The lack of privacy, and the complete awareness of the situation, could lead to better outcomes than privacy might have created.

Ironically, in a completely open society, context-shame could even effectively become an effective mechanism for reducing vindictive context-shame. Staying with the same example of an individual with a bladder control problem stemming from a medical condition, imagine a callous person mocks them. In an open world (without privacy), all other adults know who the attacker is— the person who mocked someone for having a medical condition. Generally, modern cultures frown on shaming an individual for something beyond their control; we dislike this behavior, because we are all potentially subject to externalities. Therefore, we can share information about someone behaving in an unpleasant manner, hold that attacker up to inspection, and treat them appropriately. The context-shame against someone acting inappropriately may reduce the self-shame of the person with the medical condition.

This does not reduce the self-shame and context-shame from all situations, of course: someone who drinks alcohol to the point of inebriation might lose control over their bladder and be mocked (context-shamed) for that. Many societies are quick to find humor in embarrassing situations that have been caused by the individual's own choices/judgment; this is not generally seen as inappropriate, because the individual brought the situation on themself. Someone who drinks to a point of loss of bladder control is seen as fair game for context-shaming. (As a potential added benefit; this kind of shaming might lead the person to refrain from drinking so much in the future, a choice that is probably best for everyone.)

Cultural Shame

Another aspect of shame is the seeming disparity of what is considered shameful in a given setting. Many shameful behaviors are dramatically culture-specific and in no way universal.

Religions, for example, are cultural subsets of humanity that vary wildly in what kinds of behavior are endorsed and which are disdained by their adherents. A muslim or Jew who enjoyed eating pork might feel shame (both self-shame from enjoying the food, and context-shame from fear of losing respect in the eyes of their peers), while a Catholic might instead not only lack shame from the same activity but actively find it a point of pride to win a bacon-eating contest. Any person who purports to be a member of a group but chooses to violate that group's precepts might feel shame and seek personal privacy to avoid at least the context-shame.

Without privacy, would rulebreakers be ostracized from those groups once their violations have been detected? It's quite possible. Another possibility is that the groups might learn that the vast majority of members have been violating the same rule on a regular basis and that the rule itself is faulty, not the people violating it. Or enough members of the original group might agree that this one rule is flawed and would band together to form a secondary group that kept all the other precepts but did not follow this one rule. The lack of privacy might create more options instead of less, for the affected people. (I'll expand more on this in Chapter 7.)

Location, Location, Location

Similarly, shame is often jurisdiction-dependent, beyond culturally dependent. Some territories have strict laws against behavior that is quite common (and perhaps even celebrated) in others.

For instance, the United States has strong prohibitions against online gambling, while the practice is legal in other parts of the world. This particular example gets even more bizarre when we realize that gambling, itself, is legal in many places in the United States, but only within particular physical buildings or vehicles (casinos and riverboats) and only in specific states, or counties or territories within those states.

Should a person (an American, specifically) feel shame for partaking in an illegal activity (online gambling) when the strictures for this activity seem so arbitrary and injudicious? Should I feel bad about being a lawbreaker if I can't conceivably grasp the purpose of the law and if I know that my actions would not be illegal if I was simply in another physical location?

With personal privacy, I might hide my illicit actions and avoid the context-shame . . . not necessarily the context-shame of being a gambler, but certainly the context-shame of being arrested in front of my neighbors, and suffering the tribulations of prosecution/conviction. Without privacy, my illegal activity would be easily known, and I could not derive the pleasures of recreational activities that have been deemed illegal. Is there any benefit to losing this kind of privacy?

Loss of privacy of this type might result in putting such laws into a stark relief: it could likely expose the fact that far more people break the law than subscribe to it, or possibly just that too many people break the law for the law to be reasonably enforced. Or this may lead to arbitrary enforcement, where a significant percentage of people break the law, but only a few are prosecuted; while this is not a net-positive benefit for a society and may degrade appreciation for the rule of law, it may lead to political and social resistance to such a law, creating an opportunity to repeal bad or unpopular laws.[2]

It might also foment more personal dissatisfaction with a particular law, where previously there was only an impersonal, nonspecific negative perception of the law for an individual ("well, I know gambling online is illegal, but I like gambling, and it's not hurting anyone, and I think the law is dumb, so I'll just do it anyway"). This could lead to more direct involvement in the political process for individuals who would otherwise not have any stake in a particular political outcome ("well, I wasn't going to vote in this election, but this one candidate is saying they'll legalize online gambling, and I'm sick of not being able to gamble, so I guess I'll get out and vote"). Increased citizen participation is hard to argue against as a positive outcome.

And, of course, trying to apply a law that is not followed by a significant percentage (or perhaps a majority) of the citizenry may simply be impossible, as the scale of lawbreakers far exceeds the personnel (both law enforcement and the courts) necessary to enforce it.[3] This might indicate that the law is not truly reflecting the will of the people and might therefore be reconsidered as having any validity. I'll address the policy benefits of ending privacy in Chapter 5.

---

[2] Or not. The US has prosecuted citizens for the use of illicit pharmaceuticals for about a century now, and arbitrary enforcement seems to be common: while some people are sentenced to prison for decades for possessing drugs, others who have possessed (and used) those drugs have become governors, Senators, and Presidents.

[3] This was the case during America's Prohibition, when alcohol was outlawed; so many people were being arrested and prosecuted for alcohol-related offenses that the courts and jails were overrun. Some judges took to dismissing cases out of hand or making a single decision for hundreds of suspects at a time. www.pbs.org/ken-burns/prohibition/unintended-consequences

Beneficial Shame, Which Might Be Harmful

All of these points notwithstanding, shame can be beneficial, and it's worth noting that a world without privacy will both still utilize shaming and may incur some detrimental effects.

For instance, as mentioned earlier in this chapter, becoming aware that your own condition is shared by many others can result in the loss of self-shame. This is extremely beneficial for people suffering from an embarrassing and/or debilitating medical condition; they can derive support and lose some of the self-esteem concerns associated with the malady.

However, this type of social resonance could also reinforce *bad* behavior, if the hostile actor enters a subset of the population that shares their own (distorted) views. As an example, a pedophile might feel self-shame at their own desires, which society has clearly indicated are wrong; however, if that pedophile were to find a group of likeminded people, the perception of their shared inclinations might tend to normalize the individual's view of themselves ("I'm not alone, there are others like me, so what I want must not be totally evil"). While this won't necessarily eliminate the context-shame (whatever number of pedophiles assemble, they will necessarily be smaller in number than the society as a whole, and society will continue to punish them if they act on these desires and are caught), this may remove some of the self-shame the members of this group feel, and this might lead to more of them considering acting on these desires.

I honestly do not know how these psychological mechanisms (the bandwagon effect, or reinforcing otherwise undesirable behavior among an in-group) operate or if there is an effect of causation in crime; this goes way beyond my area of expertise. However, I could reasonably foresee the potential for such an effect if all self-shame were eliminated. Still—the loss of privacy (and the attendant total access to knowledge) should mitigate any potential related dangers, because while the participants in such a group might find validation, their activity (good or ill) would still be known to others.

And context-shame is not, as a social tool, entirely bad. Earlier in this chapter, I used the example of someone mocking an elderly person for a medical condition beyond their control and how public knowledge of the person who ridiculed the elderly sufferer would result in activity that counteracts the attacker. Obviously, this could also include context-shaming them ("You made fun of an elderly person with a medical condition? You're a monster," etc.). Loss of privacy/secrecy does not preclude the use of shame, but it may reduce the *need* for it.

There are other elements of shame that are useful, though, and these could actually play a role in enhancing the benefits of losing privacy and decrementing the ill effects. For instance, if everyone is aware of the totality of everyone else's actions, crime plummets, as all potential criminals are aware that they will be observed/caught (I will discuss this more in Chapter 7). And shame is often used by close associates (friends and families) as a persuasive tool when trying to influence members of that social circle; while this is not always employed optimally or with the best of intent, it is preferable to other tools used in human history as a means of endorsing a specific choice (many of which included outright force).

For instance, consider the example of a person entering into a romantic relationship with someone who is harmful to them in a variety of ways, demonstrating parasitic, manipulative, abusive, and other troublesome qualities. That person's inner social circle recognizes the problem and signals this in a range of manners that involve both self-shame and context-shame. This is likely to include facial expressions, avoiding conversations about the partner, no longer inviting you to gatherings, not attending the events that you host, openly criticizing the partner and the relationship, and severing all communication with their former friend entirely. They are trying to encourage an outcome that they feel is best for the person (breaking up with the partner) and using shame to both convey the message and as the incentive.

This type of behavior (and use of shaming) already exists (and, indeed, pre-existed the concept of personal privacy) and will exist after privacy is gone. Interestingly, loss of privacy might make this tool both more effective and more objective.

Too often, the person who the associates are trying to convince will ignore this counsel and instead become more committed to the bad partner ("oh, they just don't know you like *I* know you; if they knew you better, they wouldn't be against you"). Without privacy, that claim will no longer have any substance; everyone will know everyone else, in the totality of their actions. There will be objective, demonstrable, calculable evidence as to how "good" or "bad" this partner is, in observable terms. This may aid the person who is the target of persuasion to see the truth about their partner.

On the other hand, it unfortunately may instead create more self-shame, as that person must face the truth that they want to be with this partner, *even though it is obvious and demonstrable that this partner is objectively bad.* The self-shame stems from the realization that the partner is detrimental, but that the person still wants the partner; this demonstrates bad judgment on their part, and the inability to use intellect and agency to transcend their emotions. I am not sure this is a net benefit, or even if it could be calculated or predicted in any way; it is simply something I consider applicable here.

Hypocrisy for Thee

There is one final potential benefit for ending shame due to privacy: ending much of the endemic hypocrisy we experience today. Hypocritical behavior thrives when one's actions do not conform to their stated beliefs. Typically, this occurs when one's self-shame conflicts with their context-shame; the individual perceives their own wants and needs to be disagreeable with their society/culture and chooses to portray themselves as acceptable to the larger population.

To echo some of the starker examples from Chapter 1, we can look at a member of the LGBTQ community in a culture/population subset that frowns on that identity. In recent American history, it has become almost a cliché that a politician or clergy member who is vocally and demonstrably concentrating on legislation and practices that deny political/legal/customary rights for gay people is later outed (often involuntarily) as being themselves gay. This type of self-shame (writ large, a form of self-loathing) seems to manifest as a driving force in how that individual's behavior conflicts with their identity: because the person believes that they, themselves, are wrong for being what the cohort (a political group or religion) prohibits, that person will over-correct their own public actions and speech to demonstrate adherence to the stated acceptable norm.

Precedents for this type of hysterical hypocrisy abound and have become so profound as to approach being a predictor as much as a trope: nobody screams more about the "dangers" and social peril of "homosexuality" as deeply self-shamed, closeted gay people.[4] (Indeed, if such a thing could be measured objectively, I'd be willing to bet that nobody is

---

[4] The expressions "wide stance" and "lift your luggage" took on new meaning in the American lexicon through follies of this type.

quite as biased and discriminatory toward any minority group as members of that group, especially those who prefer to disavow membership and attempt to pass as a member of the majority.)

Many people revile hypocrisy in any form, but it may be most troubling in the political sphere, where it can lead to statutes that create significant damage and harm to those who must live under those edicts. I will address this danger, and similar effects of privacy-related problems, in Chapter 5.

Simply put, *without privacy there can be no hidden hypocrisy.* Nobody can reasonably pretend to believe something they actually do not, if everyone can observe everyone else's behavior.

5

A Case Against Privacy: Better Policy/Practices

"I know what you're thinking about, but it isn't so, nohow. Contrariwise, if it was so, it might be; and if it were so, it would be; but as it isn't, it ain't. That's logic."
—*Dashiell Hammett, quoting Alice In Wonderland, in Citizen Cohn, by David Franzoni*

In Chapter 2, I discussed how privacy/secrecy can lead to police abuses of citizens and how lack of privacy/secrecy can also protect police from distorted/malicious false accusations. There's another aspect to privacy that harms society overall: bad policy based on private data, or data that has been influenced by privacy concerns (both direct and indirect privacy impacts on the creation of sound policy). In this chapter, I'll discuss three types of detrimental behaviors and societal effects.

- Policy based on bad data/assumptions, for police in the United States handling dog encounters
- Policy based on bad data/assumptions due to privacy/shame, for medical providers, law enforcers, and community members in the United States regarding gay people
- Concern for privacy by medical professionals that leads to creating bad datasets that affect public records and further leads to the potential for bad policies

Policy Based on Bad Data: US Police and Dogs

In the United States, police encounters with dogs often lead to the police officers shooting dogs; the US Department of Justice estimates that thousands of cases of deadly or unnecessary force against dogs are alleged each year.[1] Journalists have addressed the subject many times, as well as documenting the tragic human consequences of this practice—many people, including children, have been killed or maimed by police officers shooting at dogs . . . often when the police arrived at the wrong location and attempted to serve a warrant meant for someone else or to search another premises.[2] According to the federal government, six American states have created laws mandating that law enforcement officers receive training to estimate the danger posed by dogs and to determine the level of force necessary to counter dog risks appropriately.[3] But is this the best way to approach the problem?

Journalist Radley Balko has covered police use of force extensively, addressing both canine and human victims of overzealous or mistaken police officers.[4] His writings were the first I've noticed that highlighted a fascinating point: police officers shooting dogs is the inevitable result in an overall policing philosophy with a foundation that suggests that *any* harm that comes to law enforcement officers is unacceptable, and therefore police should employ deadly force immediately and decisively. Repeated for effect: if the fundamental policy says, "police should never be harmed," then police will use overwhelming force as a first resort.

I am not sure of the source for this approach to policing. I do, however, understand it: there is a rationale (typically presented by law enforcement officers or authorities) that suggests if police receive training that makes them reluctant to employ deadly force, then the result will be more dead police (and potentially more dead/injured citizens, because police did not react with appropriate force soon enough). This, then, might lead to recruitment and staffing problems for police forces (too many dead law enforcement officers, and it may become difficult to acquire more candidates of sufficient quality).

Is this a data-driven rationale? I seriously doubt it; such data would have to demonstrate that (a) dogs pose a constant, deadly threat to people and (b) there is no way to counter a dog attack short of killing the dog. I don't think this data exists, for one very good reason: we have counterexamples.

Balko is often quoted as pointing out that workers in other jobs (not police) deal with dog encounters on a regular basis, but only police seem

---

[1] cops.usdoj.gov/RIC/Publications/cops-w0881-pub.pdf

[2] www.counterpunch.org/2019/03/22/the-growing-epidemic-of-cops-shooting-family-dogs

[3] cops.usdoj.gov/RIC/Publications/cops-w0881-pub.pdf

[4] www.cato.org/people/radley-balko

to have a special fear of dog attacks (and only police are allowed to use deadly force); postal carriers, for instance, are attacked by dogs on a regular basis (6,244 were attacked in 2018 alone[5]), some of them quite seriously (although fatal attacks seem rare; web searches for combinations of the terms *postal carrier*, *death*, *dog attacks*, and various arrangements of these words, yield far more stories of postal carriers killing dogs than vice versa, and stories about postal carriers being killed by dog *owners*). How does the postal service deal with the threat of dog attacks, as opposed to the typical police policy? With specific training for postal carriers, in recognizing threatening dog behavior, bite avoidance techniques, and use of nonlethal technologies.[6]

Utterly anecdotally, I have seen this in action: completely due to my own negligence, two dogs in my possession lunged at a public works employee who was in my front yard inspecting a sewer drain. In this case, the person would have been totally justified killing the dogs; both animals were large, barking and growling ferociously, and traveling toward her at a high rate of speed—they gave every indication they posed a grievous risk of immediate physical harm to her. From an awkward position (she was down on the ground on her hands and knees to inspect the drain), with almost no warning, the woman drew a canister of pepper repellent from her belt and sprayed both dogs effectively. Both dogs instantly withdrew and were incapacitated for a brief time. In a situation that could have resulted in harm or death to either the dogs or the person involved, the woman's response instead culminated in no lasting harm at all to any of the participants.

What's the point of this content, in the context of a book about privacy? I want to underscore the dangers of policy based on bad data in order to further discuss how privacy creates bad data, which drives bad policy. The stark results of police policy related to dogs (which can and has led to shootings and deaths of other nearby people,[7] [8] [9] including other police officers[10]) demonstrate this point perfectly.

---

[5] about.usps.com/news/national-releases/2018/pr18_025.htm

[6] about.usps.com/news/national-releases/2018/pr18_025.htm

[7] www.cbsnews.com/news/arlington-police-shooting-body-cam-video-cop-accidentally-killing-maggie-brooks-shooting-at-dog

[8] www.dispatch.com/article/20150619/NEWS/306199744

[9] www.nbcnews.com/news/us-news/mississippi-police-fatally-shoot-man-wrong-house-while-serving-warrant-n786681

[10] valdostatoday.com/news-2/region/2020/07/officer-accidentally-shot-in-pit-bull-attack

Is it possible that police policies that encourage use of deadly force against dogs have reduced the number of officers and citizens harmed or killed by dog attacks? It's possible. But it's also likely that the number of people (including police officers) who have been killed or wounded by police use of force in countering dogs has been higher than whatever harm would be caused by dogs.

Moreover, it seems like a wildly disproportionate/misapplied use of resources/training to address a specific problem (harm/deaths of police officers); in 2017, for example, more police officers committed suicide than were killed in the line of duty.[11] Police departments would better serve their officers by training them how to identify and counter suicidal inclinations than to fear and shoot dogs.

I'll come back to the subject of suicide later in this chapter, as well.

Policy Based on Bad Data: The DSM

Using another echo of earlier themes in this book, it's interesting to examine how privacy, self-shame, and context-shame informed recent medical policies/practices in the United States regarding the gay community. In earlier chapters, I addressed how government policy and organizational trust goals were negatively affected by cultural mores and social cues about gay identity. In this chapter, I'm exploring something else: the practice and fundamental understanding of medicine. What makes this facet of privacy-based outcomes especially horrifying and fascinating is that medicine is supposed to be based on science and therefore (theoretically) devoid of subjective influences (such as morality, religion, politics, culture, and so forth). Medicine based on anything other than objective results is not science and will be demonstrably less efficacious, necessarily increasing human harm (or decreasing human benefit) as a whole.

According to its website, the American Psychiatric Association (APA) is the leading professional organization for psychiatry in the world, with members in more than 100 countries.[12] Among many other activities,

[11] www.lawenforcementtoday.com/police-suicides-outnumber-line-of-duty-deaths
[12] www.psychiatry.org/about-apa

the APA has published the Diagnostic and Statistical Manual of Mental Disorders (DSM) since 1952; the current edition, released in 2013, is known as the DSM-5. The DSM is used globally as a resource for psychiatric and other medical practitioners to recognize, diagnose, and treat mental disease and dysfunction.

For more than 20 years since its original publication, the DSM listed "homosexuality" as a mental disorder (first as a "sociopathic personality disturbance," then as a "sexual deviation," in the DSM-1 and DSM-2, respectively).[13] There is good evidence to believe that the medical practitioners at the time, the "experts" in the field, concurred with this assessment . . . even those who were themselves gay.[14]

What evidence led them to this conclusion? What data supported these policies/practices? Much of it seems to be correlation, not causation. Meaning, the data used to make the determination showed a relationship between a trait, a condition, and/or a behavior, but not that any of them caused one or the others.

This is classical fallacious reasoning; the famous example of this fallacy is to take two data points—the current outside temperature and the number of ice cream trucks in a neighborhood—and graph them in a relationship. Both numbers seem to rise and fall more or less in concert. However, drawing the conclusion that ice cream trucks make a neighborhood warmer is patently ridiculous; the two data sets are correlated, but there is no causal relationship either way.[15] In the APA's classification of "homosexuality" as a mental disease, it's likely that conditions associated with context-shame (depression, suicidal ideations, etc.) were blamed on the subjects' sexual orientation, as opposed to being correlated with it.[16]

This irrational and deleterious use of data (or lack of data or bad data or interpretation of data) almost certainly led to or supported the formulation of harmful laws, policies, and medical procedures, not the least of which were mentioned earlier in this book (the military's ban on and punishment of gay people, the government's use of gender identity

---

[13] www.ncbi.nlm.nih.gov/pmc/articles/PMC4695779

[14] www.thisamericanlife.org/204/transcript

[15] Except in the downstream causality of: hot weather brings more people outside, people want to cool off, eating ice cream to cool off is enjoyable, ice cream truck owners want to sell ice cream to people.

[16] www.ncbi.nlm.nih.gov/pmc/articles/PMC4695779

to inform trustworthiness), and some that have not yet been listed, including state and municipal "vice" laws and programs that persecuted and prosecuted gay people (for, well, being gay), medical "treatments" designed to "correct" the sexual orientation of the subject, and a general legal prejudice against anyone who might be gay. If the DSM wasn't the main reason for these policies and laws, it was certainly used to justify them.

Moreover, it's worth noting that for many jurisdictions, the legal standard for a medical diagnosis of a mental disorder is unique compared to all other medical practices, in that it is purely subjective; a person is determined to have a mental illness on the opinion of a medical practitioner (or sometimes two). This is unlike, say, the objective determination that a bone is broken (in a compound fracture, the bone protrudes from the skin) or that someone is infected with a particular bacteria (the bacteria are visible, objectively, in an enhanced view of the patient's blood sample). If the government's view of a particular person (and relationship with that person, via the court system) is based entirely on a third party's subjective assessment, and the tools for making that assessment were based on the terrible data and practices of the DSM, then the individual's handling and relationship with their own government was constantly in jeopardy and entirely at the whim of another person, creating a horrible power disparity.

It would be impossible to calculate the harm caused by this abomination of "science." I think it is incredibly worthwhile, however, to realize that without privacy, the faulty research/data that led to the tragic conclusion, as well as the prominence of the assertion itself ("homosexuality is a mental disease") would likely have been avoided and the effects attenuated.

These are a few aspects of how privacy probably harmed the interest of science and human rights during this period of the DSM.

- Test subjects/case studies had to be drawn from a pool of people willing to self-identify as members of a group that, at the time, was subject to a severe degree of context-shame. With no other motivation to participate, anyone who might fear context-shame because of their sexual orientation would likely opt to not participate, depriving the research of valid data inputs (e.g., secret gays who were *not* suffering any mental diseases). Effective research and the use of control groups will be discussed more in Chapter 7.

- Research data about a generic sample (100 random people) that indicated any given subject participated in sexual acts with same-sex partners had to rely on truthful answers from a population that was highly aware of the context-shame (and self-shame) associated with those acts. Anyone existing purely as a private gay person (as opposed to living openly/publicly, which was much rarer at the time) would be necessarily less inclined to answer truthfully.

  Coincidentally, this data (correct or otherwise) would have to be solicited under an explicit promise of privacy to suggest even the faintest possibility that the subjects would answer honestly. This actually *reduces* the overall assurance/accuracy of the data. The participants likewise have no reason to answer truthfully, as they know that any incorrect answers will never be directly associated/traced back to them, specifically, and have no additional benefit to answer honestly.

- Many of the subjects of the case studies likely either presented as desiring a change of their sexual orientation (at that time, much medical effort was put toward "curing" people of being gay) or were presented to the clinician for the same goal (by parents/ guardians of gay minors); patients subjected to medical procedures for their "illness" would necessarily seek privacy for their natural sexual orientation, and learn (or be conditioned) to present a false front to their attending doctors and researchers, thus skewing the data and results.

- As I mentioned in the previous chapter, hypocrisy cannot readily exist without privacy; if they had not been able to hide their orientation, the gay doctors/researchers who suffered self-shame and feared context-shame could not have contributed to the continuation of the awful dictates of the DSM.

It (ideally) could rightly be assumed that lack of privacy, and the attendant total openness of human sexuality, would lead to the cessation of any action (medical or otherwise) that tried to adversely label or criminalize any particular sexual practice (short of those that preclude informed consent). Simply put, if everyone knew everyone else's sexual orientation and sexual practices, then it would be obvious that sexual orientation does not indicate or result in ill effects to a specific person.

The APA finally changed the DSM after more than 20 years of brutal stupidity. This evolution, however, was not the result of new research or corrections to data or a novel scientific approach that revealed the faulty prior work; it was, instead, the result of political efforts both internal and external to the APA. Internally, a small group of heroic, gay practitioners campaigned for the modification (some openly, some not). Externally, public demonstrations and protests by activists directed at the APA almost certainly swayed a significant amount of opinion within the members of the group.

I want to be perfectly clear: this was the right conclusion, the only good and moral route for the APA to take—classifying "homosexuality" as a disease was nothing short of evil. However, *the decision to change the DSM was not science*, and changing bad doctrine because of political activism is just as shortsighted as creating bad doctrine based on bad data and religious/moral/social mores. In fact, in trying to bury the shame of its past, the APA has likely overcorrected, in that any practitioner simply researching sexual "conversion" therapy is subject to censure by the APA.

Again, I need to repeat: I find the idea that any sexual orientation or sexual interaction that incorporates informed consent could be considered a medical condition (or thereby subject to "change" by medical "treatment") ridiculous and horrible. However, closing off an avenue of research because of *any* consideration other than scientific infeasibility or the irrefutability of previous research is antithetical to science, personal freedom, and human development. If something is wrong (and I, personally, believe disease-diagnosis of nonharmful sexuality is definitely wrong), then *prove* it's wrong, with good data and good science, not by dictate.

Bad Data Derived from Concern for Privacy: Suicide

Another problem with having a society that respects privacy (and contains social mores that involve shame for biological matters) is the high degree of probability that the act of acquiring data might be tainted by reporting sources that have adjusted the content. This purposefully distorted data might then be used to craft public policies, legislation, and other outcomes (similar to the APA's bad medical standards mentioned in the previous section).

For instance, the act of suicide has traditionally been considered shameful in the United States, which might affect the accuracy of data collected about deaths in this country. Before addressing that in more detail, it's worth noting that this subject is a perfect example of how social/cultural/religious/national mores differ wildly and how morality/ethos is far from universal. This is even true within a given culture, depending on circumstance; while many specific groups within the United States might view suicide as shameful, many of these same groups admire the altruistic notion of self-sacrifice: that a human being would willfully die for another. The act might be the same (or very similar)—someone chooses to do something that will most likely result in their own death—but the cause (or perceived cause) of the dead person's choice will create a very divergent view of the act for living people reflecting on the result.

A person who died while engaged in autoerotic asphyxiation is viewed with prurient fascination tinged with public gestures of horror ("Did you hear *how* that person died?"), while a person who dies while throwing themselves between an orphan and a shark is deemed heroic. Obviously, this is almost certainly because of the perceived value of the goal of the action; accomplishing a single self-inflicted orgasm versus saving the life of a child. Still, this disparity in perspective seems to exist even when the intended results are not so stark and when the societal benefit is not nearly as apparent: a soldier throwing themselves on a grenade to save comrades is seen as heroic, even when the war that the individual soldiers are fighting is an act of evil aggression against a more-sympathetic enemy (I'm imagining a German soldier during World War II not taking the action in order to serve the Reich but acting out of obligation to comrades-in-arms and friends).

This cultural adulation of self-sacrifice is demonstrated and repeated throughout much of American literature and other popular media, even while other forms of suicide are frowned upon or outright reviled and, in some jurisdictions, even outlawed (with the comi-tragic result of the thought that it's one of the few crimes you can't be prosecuted for if you're successful). This cultural imperative cascades down from self-sacrifice/suicide (the highest order of effect—death) to recreational acts of self-harm, from cutting to smoking cigarettes (and which can also influence data-gathering, as I'll discuss later in this section).

Counting Suicides

How does this affect data collection and therefore subsequent policy?

Knowing the context-shame associated with a particular act/practice, it's easy to imagine how misreporting would occur in any number of ways, for any number of reasons.

- The surviving members of the deceased's family might not want to believe that their relative chose to perform the act; the survivors might feel guilt that they did not recognize the situation or intervene successfully in some way, and change the narrative of the death, instead.
- The surviving members of the deceased's family might not want anyone *else* to know that their relative committed suicide, for reasons related to context-shame (religious, cultural, etc.). From the abstract of a 2017 Centers for Disease Control (CDC) study in the United States: "Undercounting [suicide] may result from stigma avoidance; legal, religious, and political pressure; and underresourcing of medicolegal death investigation systems, among other reasons."[17]
- The surviving members of the deceased's family might not want the immediate/extended family's children to know the truth about their relative's death, for reasons similar to those already listed, but also because the topic of suicide, in American society, leads to many painful and difficult questions that adults prefer not to discuss with children.
- An authoritative recordkeeper (a person belonging to whichever legal entity is responsible for recording/reporting cause of death in that jurisdiction) might be sympathetic to the family's reaction to a suicide, for all the reasons already listed and more, and therefore might be inclined/persuaded to report the death as something other than suicide. As the lead author of a 2015 UK study on suicide, Professor Colin Pritchard noted: "Essentially, when a death occurs, coroners have to decide whether the death was suicide—which could be hurtful to the family—or whether it is an accident or give Open Verdict because they could not decide which. It is then categorized in World Health Organisation (WHO) stats as an Undetermined Death (UnD) and it is amongst UnD that under-reported suicides are more likely. As an UnD method of dying is very

---

[17] ajph.aphapublications.org/doi/10.2105/AJPH.2017.303863

similar to how people kill themselves it is probably the source of underreported suicide."[18]

■ Researchers with a desired outcome (that is, a preference for data that supports their hypothesis) may be more inclined to categorize/characterize particular deaths as something other than suicide (or vice versa; categorize/characterize non-suicide deaths as suicides) to achieve that outcome. Two examples that demonstrate this idea.

■ Researchers in favor of gun-control legislation might characterize suicides using firearms as "victims of gun violence," even though that specific wording can obviously mislead the audience to think that the deaths included in the data do *not* include suicides. That is to say, even though referring to someone who died by suicide as a "victim" is grammatically correct, in common American speech using the term "victim of violence" typically suggests death at the hands of another person, or a murder. This is further complicated by legal terminology/practices in many American jurisdictions, where any death other than natural causes or accident is termed "homicide," including suicide, even though common understanding of the word usually equates "homicide" with "murder," and not "suicide."

■ Researchers in favor of gun rights might purposefully not include suicides using firearms in a data set of "gun violence" in order to downplay the statistical potential for accidental fatalities involving guns. Handling data for these categories could be particularly troubling for researchers (and those entities that fund research) when tabulating teen suicides using firearms, because suicide, children, and guns are such emotionally evocative topics. (Absent the gun, would the child have died? Did the presence of the gun cause the child to suicide? Would the child have committed suicide without a gun? Did the child commit suicide, or was this an accident involving a gun?)

---

[18] www.sciencedaily.com/releases/2015/04/150407123056.htm

While these are all posited as possible theoretical reasons why suicides could be misreported, there is actually a wide body of substantiation that documents historical misrepresentation.[19] [20] [21]

Motivation and Reaction

Even beyond context-shame, there are other motivators that could cause misrepresentation of suicide, such as perverse incentives that in some way reward categorizing the act as something other than suicide. For instance, if an insurance underwriter will not pay a life insurance claim when the cause of death is suicide, then, well . . . it's in the beneficiary's financial interest to have the death listed as something other than suicide; it is, quite clearly, a situation where someone is being paid to have the death *not* be a suicide.[22] This can also occur when certain benefits are proffered or withheld because of the nature of the death (for example, in certain strict religious sects, corpses cannot be buried in graveyards if they resulted from suicide).

Another motivator (beyond context-shame and perverse incentives) might be the criminalization of aiding in the act itself; a doctor or family member providing euthanasia services to a person (in what is currently often referred to as "assisted suicide") would have every reason to fear repercussions (which could include murder charges) for doing so and would therefore be inclined to misreport the activity.

Privacy/secrecy, then, allows and creates fertile ground for misinformation; with confidentiality as to cause of death, and the opportunity for propagating convenient lies, inaccurate and misleading data can be entered into the record. Why is this troublesome? That is, why should anyone other than the aggrieved families care about the true nature of a given person's death?

---

[19] De Leo D. Can we rely on suicide mortality data? Crisis. 2015;36(1):1–3.

[20] Breiding MJ, Wiersema B. Variability of undetermined manner of death classification in the US. Inj Prev. 2006;12(suppl 2):ii49–ii54.

[21] Rockett IRH. Counting suicides and making suicide count as a public health problem. Crisis. 2010;31(5):227–230.

[22] For clarity: most modern American life insurance policies from recognized companies will pay claims even for a suicide death, as long as the death occurs at some time removed from the start of the policy (often six months to two years). It seems that while insurers do not want to incentivize suicide, they also do not want to be perceived as uncaring or unwilling to provide benefits to survivors of people who have committed suicide.

Harvesting and publishing bad data is problematic because it can lead to a misapprehension of the very situation we are trying to examine through the use of the data. Also, previously private circumstances that are now socially acceptable (i.e., those that have lost the context-shame they used to have) can affect reporting dramatically and thereby induce panic or otherwise influence results.

For instance, the US Centers for Disease Control (CDC), the federal agency responsible for determining sources and treatments of diseases and their vectors, suggest that suicide rates rose during the period 1999–2016.[23] But what if suicide rates didn't increase? What if, instead of suicide occurring more often, the *reporting* of suicide became more prevalent during that period? Could that possibly happen?

I think it's entirely reasonable to consider other externalities that may have a bearing on why suicide might be more accurately reported in 2016 than in 1999. In just that short span of time, the massive context-shame associated not just with suicide but with one of the common precursors of suicide, clinical depression, has been reduced drastically; beyond that, there is much, much less social stigma associated with even seeking medical therapies (counseling, treatment, drugs, etc.) for mental issues today than a generation or two ago.[24] So, the data the CDC is using might not actually reflect an increase in the rate or number of suicides, but instead an increase in the *rate of accurate suicide reporting*. This is intensely important, because the reporting of the topic, and the numbers associated with it, inform how we perceive the scale, scope, and nature of the very idea of suicide.

If the rate is truly increasing, this suggests that suicide is a massive problem, one that should concern almost every citizen, as the numbers of suicide deaths are accelerating at an alarming pace. If so, many more Americans are killing themselves now than we did before, then this might be an epidemic of self-inflicted death, and we need to determine what is causing it and how to stop it before we all end up killing ourselves. This would truly be a topic worth panicking about, and we should all encourage and support concentrating vast resources at finding both the causes and solutions to suicide.

---

[23] www.cdc.gov/vitalsigns/suicide/index.html
[24] In the recent past, visiting a medical practitioner for mental issues could result in a wide variety of social, legal, and professional consequences; to even admit a problem, much less to seek help for it, was a mark of shame bordering on the taboo.

If, however, the observed increase in reported suicides is due instead to greater accuracy of reporting and the rate has always been the same, then a diversion and concentration of attention and funding for suicide prevention and treatment might not be so urgent—yes, we'd like to address suicide as a human circumstance, but it's not an existential and novel immediate threat to the entire population.

In fact, if the change in reporting accuracy demonstrates that true rates of suicide have not changed in approximately 20 years, this suggests another urgent need, instead: to re-examine medical practices surrounding the treatment of pre-suicidal patients, and how they have not seemed to beneficially combat suicide to the point that suicide rates would *decline* over a period where medical treatment has become less shameful and more prevalent. That is to say, the data would suggest current medical treatments *do not work* in preventing suicide. We already know some treatments for, specifically, depression, have the horrific and awfully ironic effect of increasing potential for suicide.[25]

There is another potential benefit to decreasing privacy and increasing the openness and availability of information. When the CDC reported the increase in suicide rates, it wasn't clear whether they had in any way corrected for potential increased reporting due to decreased stigma. If we lived in a society where all information was openly accessible, it would be possible for anyone to more easily identify how that information was gathered and assess its strengths and weaknesses. The ambiguity and uncertainty around it would be removed.

This, then, is a situation where *reduction* in privacy leads to better understanding of the nature and degree of a certain threat: as context-shame surrounding depression and/or suicide decreases, the need for privacy proportionally declines, and reporting becomes more accurate, better reflecting the extent and amount of suicides.

Famous Suicide

Another situation where desire for personal privacy conflicts with popular understanding of a topic is the phenomenon of deaths of celebrities, in which the celebrity had a hand in causing the death. In these circumstances, the family of the dead celebrity might, for whatever reason, decline to share details of the life of the celebrity just before

---

[25] www.ncbi.nlm.nih.gov/pmc/articles/PMC3353604

the death, or the details of how that death occurred, citing a request to "respect the family's privacy."

In American culture, the request of a family member of someone who recently died is publicly treated with respect; it is considered impolite to impinge on such a request. However, American culture also features an intrusive urge to feast on the details of deaths, particularly those involving celebrities, with a frenzy approaching that of necrophilia. An individual American would say among others that aggressively soliciting information from someone whose family member has just died is distasteful, but that same American will gleefully pore over the grisly specifics of that death, either rumored or true, *among the same group of listeners.*

Ignoring for the moment the unabashed oddity of the family of someone who made a career being in the public eye now asking for that eye to be blinded, how does that family's "privacy" affect overall common understanding of suicide? Referring back to the earlier discussion of cultural merits and how self-sacrifice is favored over self-gratification, public opinion can often be swayed or influenced by anecdotal evidence, especially when the cases used to make the argument feature only incomplete or biased evidence in favor of a given agenda or effect.

I'll use an example of two celebrities, both who died through actions they took themselves, and the public reaction to those deaths. Celebrity A died of strangulation in a hotel room while engaged in a sexual act with a prostitute. Celebrity B died of strangulation in his own home, after a long illness.

Public response to Celebrity B's death included poignant expressions of adulation, cries for "more attention" to be paid to mental illness in general and depression specifically, and reminders that everyone be aware of the "warning signs" of suicide and how to respond to anyone you might consider suicidal. Some people suggested that this death be a springboard for legislation and public funding for anti-suicide efforts.

Public response to Celebrity A's death seemed limited to prurient repetition of the details and speculation on additional aspects of the celebrity's sexual practices. Nobody suggested creating a public policy that mandated prostitutes receive first aid/medical response training, or spread awareness on how to tie better knots. Granted, Celebrity B was more famous and had a wider audience appeal than Celebrity A.

Here's the significant problem with the dichotomy: from a privacy perspective, masking the details of Celebrity B's case allowed the story to be used, anecdotally, as a cautionary tale about the dangers of depression/ mental illness. In actuality, Celebrity B was suffering a terrible degenerative neurological condition, and suicide was a permanent release from the horrors and pain of impending total loss of brain function, preceded by the inability to perform basic bodily functions, much less the capability to perform at the levels of mastery of art Celebrity B had demonstrated up to that point. Celebrity B, then, made a conscious decision to end his own suffering before being incapacitated to the point where such a choice would not be possible; this was *not* the end result of some lifelong depressive condition.

The family's request for privacy originally following Celebrity B's death obscured the true nature of the situation and caused public discussion (and a bit of outcry) about a topic totally unrelated to the actual reason for suicide. In a totally transparent society, this would not have occurred and would not have misaligned public conversation.

Moreover, subsequent the post-mortem diagnosis, the celebrity's family tried to call for public support for the *actual* condition the celebrity suffered . . . and this has not gotten nearly the attention that earlier responses related to the topic of depression had received. It can be difficult, if not impossible, to walk back an incorrect narrative, after public perception has already coalesced and become part of the societal mythology. In a transparent society, there would be no false narrative surrounding Celebrity B's death, and therefore no undue attention paid to another condition; if people wanted to respond to B's actual condition by contributing resources or became more aware of potential symptoms through increased public interest in B or sought specific diagnoses related to that condition, then money, effort, and time might be directed toward the intended target, and not an unrelated condition.

Jumping on Guns and Bandwagons

This same phenomenon, fraudulent narratives becoming ingrained "truth," can happen at a micro level as well as the macro. In another completely anecdotal example, I have known adults who had malformed opinions about the safety/risk associated with a certain technology because of a family legend created to assuage the sensibilities of the children involved at the time of the inciting incident. The story went like this: decades before the adults I knew had been born, when their relatives (aunts and uncles) were young, they had been playing, as children do, in a room where a firearm was kept. The children were jumping up and down on the bed, not knowing that a gun was kept underneath it; the jumping caused the gun to go off, and another passing relative (adult at the time) was killed by the shot.

This story does not withstand even the barest rational scrutiny. The combination of wildly unlikely factors (a gun being triggered completely accidentally without even being directly touched by a person, another person walking by at exactly the unfortunate moment, the shot miraculously hitting the victim without being aimed, the accidental/unaimed shot being so unluckily accurate as to be fatal) suggest another, far more likely set of circumstances: while playing, the children discovered the gun, were handling it, aimed it a relative, accidentally fired it, and killed that person. The family, to protect the children (from a variety of effects, including self-shame and legal repercussions), misrepresented the facts of the situation, to the point where the story became truth to subsequent generations. The adults I knew, descendants of the children involved, were so convinced that a gun can be fired in such a way (children jumping in its proximity) that they had an irrational fear and dread of being in the same building where they knew a gun to be. Personal privacy, in this case, while intended to protect children from a harmful reality, led to disinformation that colored the world for subsequent generations. That's a recurring and all-too-predictable result of privacy/secrecy.

A total lack of privacy would then, rationally, lead to better collection and distillation of data and therefore better understanding not only from a popular perspective, but also among clinicians and policymakers who are attempting to address the underlying concerns.

But I'd be remiss if I also didn't mention here that removing privacy is not a panacea for social and human perils; in fact, this topic yields an opportunity to discuss novel and emergent risks associated with the decline of privacy. These include the bandwagon and copycat effects. To continue the previous section's topic of suicide, it is quite possible that additional transparency might actually lead to the societal harm of marked increase in suicide rates, due to both the bandwagon and copycat effects.

Let's start with the bandwagon effect: the phenomenon where knowledge that some people are participating in a certain activity encourages others to participate as well. This is commonly used for marketing purposes. With suicide and other forms of self-harm, wider exposure and knowledge of the practice might decrease inhibitions that would otherwise prevent someone from choosing to commit suicide. As context-shaming aspects of a society are reduced and a particular behavior seems less fraught with negative impact, the potential for an individual to opt for suicide might increase.

In fact, a certain popularity surrounding the practice might emerge, particularly among specific groups within the society as a whole (for instance, younger adults/teens). As self-harm/suicide takes on the mantle of "trendy," some people who would otherwise not have considered that choice might add it to a list of possibilities. Ironically, the bandwagon effect may be increased by the very efforts used to dissuade the target audience from engaging in harmful behavior; in an absurd twist, *the education/information effort might be the exposure that causes the audience to choose that behavior.*[26] Moreover, even just hearing about a certain practice for the first time may make it appealing; 40 years ago, there was not much documentation of the behavior known today as "cutting" among young people— currently, news articles and "expert" opinion pieces declare the incidence of teen cutting to be escalating (often using terms of hysteria, such as "alarming" and so forth). This may be an example of behavior propagating itself.

Then there is the concept of the copycat effect. It is conceivable that when people have heard that someone has committed suicide, the option of taking their own life seems more appealing (or less shameful). This is probably more true for young people and others who are particularly impressionable, and the effect may be heightened when the suicide involves either someone famous or otherwise relatable to the person considering the suicide (someone in the same age group, location, or

---

[26] There's some controversy as to outcomes, but this may have happened with the American behavior-modification program for schools known as DARE in the 1980s–1990s. DARE was designed to decrease the demand for illicit drugs by young people, through educating students about the effects and consequences of drug use. It may have, instead, had no effect on drug use at all, and some reports suggest it may have *increased* students' initial experimentation with drugs. There seems to be no strong evidence that the program decreased student drug use. Anecdotally, I clearly recall that the teenager who offered me marijuana during my first day of high school proudly displayed a DARE "Hugs—Not Drugs!" bumper sticker on his car.
priceonomics.com/dare-the-anti-drug-program-that-never-actually
and/www.crimesolutions.gov/ProgramDetails.aspx?ID=99

similar demographic).[27] This concept is so prevalent in the literature that it has been termed "the Werther effect."[28] This phenomenon suggests that total transparency (a lack of privacy regarding suicide in particular) might not reduce the number or rate of suicides. However, there is some suggestion that the *way* the information is communicated might impact the overall suicide rate, or at least the way someone chooses to suicide; reporting guidelines published in Austria may have been beneficial in reducing the number of suicide attempts in the Vienna subway system.[29]

So, common knowledge of actual suicide rates/numbers/incidents might not reduce overall suicides/attempts/rates. Privacy, or lack of privacy, is not a magical solution to every risk facing humanity. I do think, however, we should enter a post-privacy world ready to collect and digest data in a meaningful, objective, rational way, truly applying scientific methodology to determine how and why to approach the dissemination of information with trepidation or hope.

---

[27] For example, four teenagers who went to the same California high school committed suicide using the same means (jumping in front of a train) over a six-month span. This is statistically wildly improbable to be a strictly random coincidence given average rates of suicide. abcnews.go.com/US/palo-alto-struggles-rash-teen-train-suicides/story?id=8881813

[28] Oddly, taken from a literary source: a work of Goethe published in 1774. en.wikipedia.org/wiki/Copycat_suicide

[29] www.ncbi.nlm.nih.gov/pubmed/18082110

6

A (Bad) Solution: Regulation

> "Of all tyrannies, a tyranny sincerely exercised for the good
> of its victims may be the most oppressive. It would be better
> to live under robber barons than under omnipotent moral
> busybodies. The robber baron's cruelty may sometimes sleep,
> his cupidity may at some point be satiated; but those who
> torment us for our own good will torment us without end for
> they do so with the approval of their own conscience . . . This
> very kindness stings with intolerable insult. To be "cured"
> against one's will and cured of states which we may not
> regard as disease is to be put on a level of those who have not
> yet reached the age of reason or those who never will; to be
> classed with infants, imbeciles, and domestic animals."
> —C.S. Lewis, God in the Dock: Essays on Theology
> (Making of Modern Theology)

So how do we, as a species, transition gracefully from a society where we (think we) desire privacy and personal secrecy, from the point where we treasure it, and jealously guard it, to a society of total openness and transparency?

I honestly have no idea. I do know it will be incredibly painful and frustrating for many individuals and probably entire groups and populations while the transformation takes place. I was raised to prize privacy enormously, then compounded that perceived value through my choices and habits, which carried over into my professional life as well. I, myself, will probably suffer personally and professionally, along with many others, if this evolution takes place during my lifetime—I see that, recognize it, and still acknowledge that the end-state results will be better for humanity and all individuals eventually. I also realize it's going to happen, regardless of any attempts to prohibit or deter it.

Moreover, I think it's pretty clear that organized efforts to retard the process will do much more harm than good and cost more than the supposed value they are intended to achieve. I think we're experiencing that now, as punitive actions related to privacy legislation and contractual obligations bleed financial damage to "violating" entities, and breaches of privacy seem to continue and escalate, both in size and pace. (In the European Union, for example, enforcement actions since the implementation of the General Data Protection Regulation [GDPR] in 2018 have cost companies the equivalent of $126 million USD, according to an industry study published in 2020,[1] and this does not reflect the additional costs of compliance, which may drive expenses that are orders of magnitude higher, across the entire market, as well as lost opportunities for consumers, because small or medium-sized businesses cannot afford the barriers to entry that these regulations create.) However, punitive fines that damage companies that have already been victimized by attackers doesn't seem to deter the criminals in any way. That should come as no surprise.

But if I didn't address the potential for "easing" the technological and sociological effects of diminishment of personal privacy through regulation, I'd be ignoring the pointed and plaintive cries from almost every angle and sector. Industry experts call for privacy regulation,[2] as do consumer groups,[3] and, perhaps least astonishing, established industry participants[4] and politicians.[5]

The problems with this approach are manifold and severe, and the most pernicious aspect of touting regulation as a "solution" is that often the ill-effects compound gradually and seem to be unobtrusive, until a specific issue has ballooned to the point where it's unavoidably noticeable and painful. As with other examples of the law of unintended consequences mentioned earlier in this book, most of these attempts to regulate personal privacy seem well-intentioned but lead to disastrous results.

---

[1] www.dlapiper.com/en/uk/insights/publications/2020/01/gdpr-data-breach-survey-2020

[2] www.cpomagazine.com/data-privacy/top-ceos-now-pushing-for-federal-privacy-legislation

[3] www.scmp.com/lifestyle/technology/article/1385959/activists-civil-society-groups-call-overhaul-governments

[4] techcrunch.com/2019/03/30/mark-zuckerberg-actually-calls-for-regulation-around-content-elections-privacy

[5] www.theglobeandmail.com/politics/article-privacy-watchdog-calls-for-stronger-laws-to-protect-canadians-digital

Regulation = Destruction

I'll begin with the dictum stated by Supreme Court Chief Justice John Marshall in 1819, somewhat parsed: that the power to regulate something is the power to destroy it . . . and that this power, when wielded, stifles creation.[6] Carrying this logic forward a few steps, the power to regulate privacy (or information, as a whole) is the power to destroy privacy (for an individual, or a group, or a population). Giving a specified power to any entity exclusively, whether that entity is a government or a business or a group of people, grants that entity an undue, unfair, unearned power over all others, and should be the absolute last resort of any possible option.

This is what baffles me about people who advocate for both freedom of information and for governmental control of the means to disseminate information; how can those two things be resolved if they are diametrically opposed? For example, in a bizarre set of circumstances, during the same time period (2011–2012), the US federal government attempted to create two programs that seem utterly contradictory.

- One program gave the US President the ability to take control of nationwide telecommunications and Internet communication; this was frequently referred to as an "Internet kill switch."[7]
- The other program was funded by the US Department of State to create and disseminate communications capabilities, including Internet service, independent from any national or political control.[8]

The justifications for both programs likewise seemed at odds: the President wanted the ability to seize control of communications

---

[6] Marshall was writing the decision for *McCulloch v. Maryland*, specifically about the government of an American state being able to tax a property (a bank) owned and operated by the federal government. www.law.cornell.edu/supremecourt/text/17/316

[7] www.cnet.com/news/obama-signs-order-outlining-emergency-internet-control

[8] www.discovermagazine.com/technology/us-state-department-backing-shadow-internet-and-cellphone-projects

infrastructure to ensure that the government could continue to exist and function during any crisis situation, and the State Department wanted to encourage foreign political dissidents and revolutionaries who might be affected when their government seized control of communications infrastructure (as had happened in several countries, including Egypt, Syria, and Bahrain, where revolutions, coups, and political resistance movements had recently occurred). So, American taxpayers were simultaneously paying for foreign dissidents to have a freedom of unfettered communication that they (the American taxpayers) could not similarly enjoy *and* for the government that prevented them from enjoying that freedom.

From what I can gather, neither program made much headway in their original forms, which may be considered fortunate or otherwise, according to your taste.

To cite a more specific example, I want to tread very carefully. Bruce Schneier is an expert I admire and respect to the utmost degree; he is much, much smarter than I am, and far more well-versed in both the practice and documentation of privacy and security matters (I wholeheartedly recommend anything he has published—he's a brilliant writer and speaker[9]). He has been a cornerstone of this field for 30 years and knows more about privacy than I could ever learn in another hundred.

However, Schneier (along with many other practitioners in our field) has constantly and continually called for increased government regulation of privacy in order to protect individual privacy from the vagaries of businesses that deal in personal information. (For clarity's sake, these businesses usually deal in personally identifiable information [PII] primarily to generate advertising revenue as a means to facilitate operations and also for profit.) Schneier is the man who coined the term *security theater* to describe security practices that appear to counter risk but actually do nothing, mostly as a reaction to American government efforts to "secure" air travel after the 9/11 attacks.[10] (The head of the Transportation Security Administration [TSA], the US federal agency that conducts these operations, unironically used the term to describe the reasons for revoking one of the more stupid, least-enforceable aspects of the TSA's program: passengers carrying cigarette lighters aboard commercial planes.[11] [12])

---

[9] Full disclosure: the publisher of this book also publishes some of Schneier's works.

[10] In his book, Beyond Fear (Copernicus, 2003).

[11] www.cbsnews.com/news/tsa-to-lift-ban-on-most-lighters-on-planes

[12] Full disclosure: I have both provided security consulting services to the TSA and violated TSA regulations by carrying lighters aboard aircraft, sometimes simultaneously.

I understand Schneier's reasoning, and I respect the logic: in a free-market system, with no prohibitions against collecting and disseminating personal information, businesses will engage in whatever activity they choose to make the most profit, including harvesting and using personal data through any and all means.

Short of some centralized control (so the reasoning goes), companies will continue to elicit and distribute users' personal data, even if the broad, long-term results do not necessarily benefit the users. For Schneier, and others of like mind, the only way to abrogate this practice and attenuate the potential negative effects is to cede control of the activity to a disinterested third party (that is, some entity that is not a company intending to profit from the endeavor, and not the individuals themselves, because individuals may not recognize the tertiary and tail-end effects of their own choices). The government, then, is the only likely candidate to have the reach and power to influence and check the ambitions of market-based data purveyors (some of which are so incredibly large and wealthy as to rival some governments in terms of scope and financial wherewithal).

I understand this rationale—I can even appreciate it, to a degree. But the massive shortcoming is an integral fault in the assumptions: there is no historical example where this power—a centralized, governmental control of a particular individual right—has ever been exercised to the betterment of the affected individuals. In fact, we have a litany of counterexamples (some of which I'll include in this chapter, momentarily). But the argument for regulation of personal privacy boils down to one essential flaw: *this* time, for *this* regulation, we'll somehow write the law so specifically and perfectly that it couldn't possibly be misinterpreted or abused, and we will pick the *right* people to administer and enforce it . . . unlike all those other examples where one or more of those pieces didn't quite function the way we thought it might.

Regulation doesn't work like that—it *can't* work like that, because statutes and lawmakers can never foresee all the permutations of what might occur or what technology might evolve or how public perception might change. And laws that are outdated still cause pain and suffering for individuals who have to live through the effects of those laws, until the old, bad laws are finally morphed or rejected. Unintended consequences always occur. Always. They are part and parcel of the regulatory process.

Why is this any worse than the current state of affairs, where the personal data of so many individuals is in the hands of large companies, bandied about by billionaires, leveraged for any and all advantage—where any breach might disclose an individual's entire life's information?

Because in a decentralized, market-based paradigm, the effects of an unauthorized breach on *me* are my choice, and the damage is necessarily contained. There is only so much that an owner/operator of a company might do to me or prevent me from doing. For instance, private companies can ban me (and have) from sharing information via their platforms or limit what I could share or when or how. I am still free, however, to use other platforms or media to express myself, in a manner I see fit. The owners of the company that refuses to engage with me cannot choose to stifle me if I go elsewhere to conduct my transaction/expression. Being kicked off one company's site does not mean I'm kicked off every site on the Internet.

More importantly, today, in the current model, I can create my own platform, if I choose. This is especially important when seemingly monolithic companies merge with or purchase their competition, and the number of viable platforms seem to decrease. If modern technology has taught us anything, it's that abilities for expression and commerce are increasingly offering democratization and egalitarian economies of scale.

Journalist AJ Liebling was famously purported to have written, "Freedom of the press is guaranteed only to those who own one." (Obviously, Liebling wrote this back when large, expensive printing presses were used to make books, magazines, and newspapers and there was not yet an Internet, much less personal computers—so Liebling meant that while it's pleasant that American law allows theoretically anyone to express themselves however they choose, the reach of your expression might be limited by the rich and powerful people who controlled the means of conveying it.)

Today, everyone owns a virtual press, or can: the number of ways you, yourself, can create a message that theoretically can reach everyone on the planet (should everyone choose to avail themselves of that message) are almost limitless, and the cost negligible. There are currently *not* a limited number of outlets or media moguls that can choke out expression such that only their messages are conveyed; residents of a city are no longer restricted to consuming data from three television channels and two daily newspapers and eight radio stations; every person on the planet is both a potential contributor and consumer of data.

With regulation, this pool dries up. When a central authority is the ultimate arbiter of what can and cannot be conveyed, there is no recourse, no way to go to a competitor to express yourself. In modern societies, governments have a monopoly on the legal use of force; if the government tells me to do something (or not do something) and I violate that rule, the government can use force against me, and I am not allowed to resist by using force in like manner. An online social media platform, however, is not legally allowed to use force; data companies do not have badges and guns and the force of law.

I also have legal recourse against a private-sector company; in the eyes of the court, me and any company/billionaire have total equanimity. (Yes, of course, the large company/billionaire can marshal far many more resources than I could, to include lawyers, investigators, and so forth—but we're on the same legal footing; we are equals as far as the court is concerned.) This is not the case with regulatory control; I might not have any legal recourse against a sovereign entity. A sovereign government might decide it cannot be sued by me, and there is next to nothing I can do about it.

Moreover, depending on the regulatory framework, a specific court might consider the parties wholly unequal when a government is involved: in the United States, regulatory bodies typically write the laws they will enforce (administrative law), employ the law enforcers, employ the prosecutors, and employ the judges of the specific court where your case will be heard if you argue with a regulator. (For example, the Federal Trade Commission [FTC] publishes administrative laws regarding consumer protection, chooses the companies the FTC will target for violations, collects evidence, and issues its own court orders, from FTC judges, that are legal and enforceable; the targeted companies may or may not be allowed to present contrary evidence, have legal representation during hearings, and/or appeal any decisions, at the FTC's discretion.[13])

---

[13] For an excellent depiction of how this system can be abused and how it dramatically stifles productive (and even life-saving) activity, in a mechanism that is highly resistant to change, I recommend Michael J. Daugherty's true story about his company LabMD, "The Devil Inside the Beltway," michaeljdaugherty.com

Legitimate Fear of the Private Sector

That is not to say that Schneier and others who call for limiting market control of data are way off-base: there is rational cause to distrust and be fearful of companies and those who run them, particularly when it comes to valuable or sensitive data.

What harm can come to you from private-sector entities and the use of data that either describes you or belongs to you? They could copy/steal it, sell it, illicitly modify it, make it public without your consent, or prevent you from disseminating it on their property. This might be a case of fraud, as happened with Enron,[14] WorldCom,[15] and Adelphia.[16] It might be outright theft, as happened with Tata Consultancy Services.[17] All of this may affect your ability to earn money from your data or get favorable credit or cause you embarrassment or affect your ability to gain employment elsewhere.

Moreover, personal choice in limiting the dissemination of our data is not as clear-cut as with other types of transactions. My exposure to risk, when sensitive/personal data is involved, is often beyond the scope of my knowledge and ability to govern, if not my ultimate control.

In most other transactions, I am familiar with the stakes involved and can make informed decisions. If I buy a hammer, I know I'm getting an object in exchange for an amount of currency. There might be risks associated with the transaction/purchase. What if I buy the hammer online and I pay the money and don't get the tool in exchange? What if the delivery takes longer than I expected? What if there's a material defect in the hammer's construction and it breaks the first time I use it? What if it's weighted wrong and I smash my thumb while using it?

I am familiar with the possible hammer-related risks and can choose to offset them through a variety of means. I might buy from a hardware store I've shopped at before, and my history of business with them carries some trust with previous experience. I might only buy from a

---

[14] www.journalofaccountancy.com/issues/2002/apr/theriseandfallofenron.html

[15] www.thebalance.com/worldcom-s-magic-trick-356121

[16] www.reference.com/world-view/happened-adelphia-scandal-40a00b6679677497

[17] health.economictimes.indiatimes.com/news/health-it/us-jury-fines-tcs-940m-for-healthcare-software-theft/51861855

manufacturer who offers a warranty on the tool or from a brand that is recognized and certified by industry standards. I might only make the purchase from a vendor that offers me a return policy.

But with data, I'm at a distinct disadvantage. In almost every transaction, part of the exchange that is not explicitly negotiated/stated is that a record of the transaction, and my part in it, is an element of the purchase price. I have little to no choice about limiting the data involved in the transaction, or any reasonable way of controlling how the data will be handled from that point onward. I usually assume that any data shared with any entity must necessarily be shared with all other possible entities (in effect, sharing it publicly), because of the aftermarket for data (or user-generated metadata). This is not a comforting notion; beyond the possibility for revelation/harm, I lose agency in each transaction.

And unlike other aspects of a transaction, limiting the informational component is not simply a matter of choosing to do without a simple or convenient option. Yes, the argument could be made, "Well, you don't have pressing, existential need for access to online social media." This is true—I could live without ever posting photos of my pets/meals/relatives/vehicles for the world to see. However, the more prosaic elements of connected existence are not the only benefits I would have to forego if I chose to limit my risk by not engaging online at all. By limiting my Internet presence, I would likewise have to severely retard my ability to engage in business networking/marketing, seeking relationships, conducting online shopping/delivery, acquiring knowledge (both mundane and crucial), facilitating financial transactions, and all the other vast benefits modern connectivity technology allows. To simply say, "stay offline, then," is disingenuous; a modern person in a modern society who opts to not participate is hampered to an exceedingly ridiculous degree—yes, it can be done, but it is dramatically harder to pursue the same level of accomplishment and success in any and all ventures if you choose not to use modern technology.

Moreover, there are secondary and tertiary data-gathering and brokering entities and activities that are next to impossible to preclude, even if one chooses to "live off the grid." All the most basic human actions—renting a living space, connecting it to power and water utilities, paying for that domicile, etc.—are being assessed and reported to other entities not party to the original transaction.

To restate this plainly, I go to rent a home, and the owner of the property, the banks (both mine and the owner's), the utility providers, and many other entities, are reporting the transactions (both the initial and the recurring payments) to third parties such as credit bureaus and government regulatory agencies, etc., with whom I have no direct association nor any way to discriminate between. Is it possible to even conduct this transaction without sharing my own data? I'm not sure—I think it may be possible, but the difficulty would be enormous and far more costly to the individual than is commensurate with the risk to and value of the associated data. I *could* find a property owner who wouldn't ask for my name and let me pay in cash . . . I *could* find some payment instrument for delivering rent that doesn't involve a bank (cash or money order, perhaps) . . . I *could* find a domicile where utilities are included in the rent payment . . . but this artificial limitation of my options is wildly disproportionate to the relative risk to me and my data. (Also, the additional other risks would be abundant; if I enter into a lease arrangement with the property owner and that agreement does *not* include my name/identification, how could I ever hope to seek legal recourse if we later had a disagreement as to details and contractual terms?)

It is basically untenable to exist in a modern society without exposing some personal data in some way, and individual volition is not the distinguishing element that it is with other types of transactions.

So, yes, I can fully grok the substance and import of an argument that suggests that market-based limitations on data usage are not feasible. I even agree with them, almost completely.

Where I break rank is making the next jump: that government regulation is the only solution to the conundrum.

Exceptions to the Rules

One of the most significant reasons to resist government regulation of privacy is the simple fact that government likes to exclude itself from the rules it makes. (This is especially true of the US federal government.) If privacy is something to truly value, to the point where secrecy is the means we agree to protect it, then everyone should be included in the limitations on collecting/processing/using privacy data.

Of course, this would make a lot of the activity that government performs either impossible or useless: law enforcement, taking the census, or even tabulating voter registration would not exist if identification and recognition of individual people were not allowed.

We see manifestations of this line of thinking even when legislation is created specifically to hamper the federal government's ability to keep data secret from its citizens: the Freedom of Information Act (FOIA) stipulates that the federal government must disclose any information requested by a citizen or resident of the United States . . . with a few exceptions. It is the exceptions that create the loophole the government can use to continue hiding information.

For instance, germane to this discussion, one of the exceptions allows for redacting the personal information of a person—if you make a request, say, to the US military for any record concerning people named "Ben Malisow," the military might deliver some documents about that person, but certain lines of text will be marked out so as to make the person's private data (such as Social Security number, home address, etc.) illegible. Other exceptions include evidence for pending legal cases, classified material that could harm "national security," trade secrets, internal personnel matters, material prohibited under other federal laws, financial information, privileged communication between agencies, and, for some reason, geological information about wells.[18]

There are enough exemptions that, should a bureaucrat be sufficiently determined, preventing the release of information would not be all that difficult, even though this is expressly counter to the entire purpose and intent of the law.

Sometimes, governmental exceptions are relatively benign, if annoying, such as when the Federal Communications Commission (FCC) interpreted federal law and implemented rules associated with "robocalls" (using automated means to call telephones) and granted an exception to politicians.[19] Other exemptions are fairly horrifying, such as when the FBI operated a child pornography website.[20]

---

[18] www.foia.gov/faq.html

[19] www.fcc.gov/political-campaign-robocalls-robotexts

[20] This was part of the awfully named Operation Pacifier, an effort to prosecute people involved in creating, distributing, and consuming child pornography. Yes, we can all agree that making or distributing child pornography is vile and that law enforcement should work to prevent it. We can even agree that evidence of the crime needs to be seized and held by law enforcement in order to present to the prosecution/court. But this is where the exception to law and good sense enters the discussion: if we agree child pornography is horrible, then the government should not grant itself the exception to distribute it, for any reason. en.wikipedia.org/wiki/Playpen_(website)

Attempts to protect personal privacy through secrecy, administered by a central authority, will be subject to exemptions like these, and the disproportionate power of government over the individual will only continue.

Chill Out

Philosophical differences will also lead to increased potential for conflict between government and the individuals constituting the citizenry. The European mindset that led to the General Data Protection Regulation (GDPR), the major international law driving a multitude of online business practices worldwide, is that personal privacy is paramount: an individual should have full control of any data elements identifying themself. The United States takes a converse view: that personal expression—the freedom of the individual to convey any and all information, in any manner the individual sees fit—is paramount. These two precepts cannot coincide: if I have the right to control my own identifying data, I can control what you say about me; if I have the right to express myself however I want, then I can release/distribute information about you.

The two approaches effectively place power in different hands: with the sanctity of expression, the government must demonstrate that there is a good purpose for limiting an individual's ability to convey information; if privacy is seen as the apex of importance, the individual would have to demonstrate sufficient reason to circumvent the law, and permission would be granted (or not) by the government.

This creates a massive disparity in power. The United States was created because individuals did not trust their government, having long suffered abuses from it. The country was purposefully constructed in such a way as to limit governmental power, for fear of what might result; the individual was viewed as the ideal unit of choice and responsibilities—the group was suspect, and the authority vested to the group abrogated. The group was prevented from imposing its will on the individual, unless there was a reason of vast importance justifying otherwise.

Europe, on the contrary, has long trusted its institutions; Europeans have seemed to favor collective decision-making over that of the individual. I am not sure why this is; given the history of European governments, there should be more than sufficient reason for individuals to distrust those institutions.

Making the government the arbiter and enforcer of which data can be conveyed, and how, is ridiculously dangerous. While the United States does not have a long history of laws concerning privacy, the country has more than enough negative examples of governmental enforcement of other laws that restrict expression.

For instance, American laws impinging on freedom of expression leave only a few circumstances where governmental intercession on public discourse are allowed. These include incitement (to violence/ panic), intellectual property protection, prohibited communications (such as the aforementioned child pornography as well as national secrets/classified information), and obscenity. (There are also statutory protections for civil actions arising from other types of expression, such as slander/libel, but these allow an individual to protect their own property, to include their public persona, from other people, and aren't criminal matters.) For one example to demonstrate the dangers of governmental control of expression, I'll use obscenity.

Historical enforcement of obscenity laws seems almost prosaic in the modern age; these governmental actions dealt almost entirely with sexually oriented ideas and images, and the idea that sex-related materials can cause individual harm is just slightly ridiculous in the age of the Internet (which is to say, if sexually-related material does, in fact, cause harm, then the entire species is doomed, just from the vast amount currently in existence). Obscenity laws have been used to control access to medical information; specifically, the Comstock laws were certainly designed to prevent women from having access to information about reproduction,[21] to include birth control methods as well as any material allowing those methods to be put into practice. Obscenity laws were also used to stifle adult entertainment, in the form of pornographic films and similar performances and media.

But perhaps the most bizarre implementation of these laws was the use of them against comedians.

Humor is a weird thing: a vast percentage of it requires understanding of culture, language, situations, and the context of the material being presented. Some humor transcends this, such as physical comedy involving only bodily motions (silent films featuring comedic performances of physical humor display this by tapping into an almost universal human knowledge of physics and interaction; even someone

---

[21] en.wikipedia.org/wiki/Comstock_laws

who has no familiarity with the culture of the film's origin can appreciate a pratfall or well-executed bit of pantomime, and almost every culture has a similar kind of theatrical tradition). What might be funny to one person could be offensive to someone else. What might be funny today might be construed as crude ten years from now (or it might even be totally misunderstood, in that it simply is not funny in the newer context). But it's difficult to imagine that someone could say something so disturbing that some people would pay to see it performed, for their own amusement, while others would want to imprison and punish the comedian through use of force.

And yet that's exactly what happened in the United States, under obscenity laws.

Lenny Bruce[22] and George Carlin[23] were stand-up comics in the United States; their careers were fairly contemporaneous; they both rose to prominence in the 1960s. Both were arrested and prosecuted for things they said publicly, during performances. Bruce was arrested numerous times, in Los Angeles, San Francisco, Chicago, and New York City, between 1961 and 1964; Carlin was arrested in Milwaukee in 1972. Prosecutors claimed Bruce had violated obscenity laws by using prohibited words and making certain gestures; Carlin was prosecuted solely for saying specific words (his performance included a routine called, "Seven Words You Can Never Say on Television," probing the arbitrary vagaries of expression, language, and communication in a government-regulated medium; in 1973, a radio station aired a recording of a version of this routine, and was fined by the FCC).[24]

---

[22] www.thefire.org/first-amendment-library/special-collections/lenny-bruce-cases

[23] markwalston.com/2012/03/18/george-carlin-utters-seven-words-and-is-arrested-for-public-obsenity

[24] Over time, Carlin's routine evolved, and he constantly updated and utilized far more than the original seven words. Adam Savage (from the TV show "Mythbusters") discusses this in his book, *Every Tool's A Hammer* (Atria, 2019). Savage reviewed every Carlin routine he could find in order to make a card catalog of all the words. Savage interprets Carlin's intent (and any fan of Carlin's work can readily recognize this point); thus: if a list of prohibited language starts at seven words, there's a real danger that the list will grow to a dozen, then two dozen, and so forth, until the listmaker (the government) has outlawed more words than it allows, and controls communication. This is another aspect of a regulatory state that Orwell predicted in *1984* (Secker & Warburg, 1949), with the concept of the Newspeak dictionary . . . which grows shorter every iteration.

That these two people were subject to arrest and prosecution is regrettable. The potential larger harm in these types of actions, though, could be tragic: that by setting a precedent and making an example of those individuals, the government was attempting to disrupt and prevent types of expression and stifle particular lines of conversation and, ultimately, thought. The kind of laws used in these prosecutions (the "obscenity" laws), and the kind of government actions the laws are used to initiate, create what the US Supreme Court has called a "chilling effect" on free thought, assembly, and expression.[25]

If it becomes commonplace for the government to arrest, prosecute, and fine or imprison people for saying certain words or making specific gestures, then people will have to carefully consider their thoughts and words before expressing themselves, for fear of punishment by force.

This is horrifically troubling for two reasons. First, this self-censorship creates a situation where thoughts and ideas are inhibited even before they enter conversation; this necessarily limits what people can talk about, or even think. This leads to creating taboos, entire subjects that nobody is willing to discuss, as those concepts become sacrosanct and unassailable. For a free people, and for humanity as a whole, this is a significant problem: good ideas should be considered good only if they are continually challenged and reproven, not because they are free from critique. We can only improve our circumstances if we are able to challenge and overturn the biases of the past and replace them with newer, better ideas—that cannot happen when we aren't allowed to challenge certain revered concepts.

Second, the tendency for legal prohibitions, and regulatory power ceded to central authority, is to grow, not to shrink. This trend can be exacerbated only when the controlled items are words and gestures. Will the central authority create a concrete list of what cannot be said? Or will it create an opposite list, of what can be said . . . and everything not listed is prohibition by exclusion? There is a frightening possibility that something might be added to the list later, after everyone has already gotten used to enforcement actions related to the original list . . . and

---

[25] This terminology was first seen in a Supreme Court decision in 1952; that case did not involve obscenity but was instead about the rights of people, particularly teachers, to freely join groups of their choosing outside the school environment. The term would also later be used by the Supreme Court in many similar findings. users.soc.umn .edu/~samaha/cases/weiman%20v%20updegraff.htm

the things added might include "disagreement with elected officials," or "mocking a certain party or candidate." This road leads to tyranny.[26]

Worse, what if there is no defined list of proscribed terms/motions, and the central authority is allowed to arbitrarily ban anything they don't like? Who will hold this power? Will it include elected officials the citizens have chosen? Appointees of those selected persons? Career bureaucrats that were never chosen or appointed, but are ensconced in their positions? Law enforcement functionaries who patrol our conversations in an attempt to detect wrongdoing?

And culture evolves: words and gestures take on new meanings, and newer words and gestures are added to our communication suite. Words that were prosaic yesterday might take on somewhat offensive meaning today . . . and become passé tomorrow.[27] Does the power to control communication grant a blank check to the authority with that power, under an acknowledgment that any word can become prohibited? (And yes, the term *blank check* is used here ironically as an example—its origins grounded in the obsolete practice of actually writing checks.)

Moreover, even cultures that use the same language will have different meanings/values ascribed to specific words/terms/gestures. Ostensibly, both the United States and the United Kingdom use English, but where you are and who you're talking to may severely affect your use of the words *bloody*, *dick*, *ass*, and so forth, and using your spread forefinger and index finger in forward motion at another person might be utterly innocuous or a grave insult. Are imported/exported media going to be free of sanction by a central authority, if the intent to

---

[26] This is not a theoretical notion or something extracted from the distant past; in 2020, the Prime Minister Viktor Orban demanded and received sweeping enhanced powers to rule Hungary, which included the ability to stifle "misinformation" about government actions (including criticism of Orban himself). Who determines what communications are "misinformation"? ipi.media/hungary-press-freedom-threatened-as-orban-handed-new-powers

[27] This kind of situation affected Beaver College, an American institution of higher learning established in 1853, when the word *beaver* was used to indicate a watergoing woodland creature that builds dams. That word would later evolve into slang for "vagina." Today, the slang usage has mostly become obsolete, and the word is largely limited to describing the animal again. This happened too late for Beaver College. nypost.com/2000/06/01/leave-it-to-beaver-college-dammed-by-name
Fans of Kurt Vonnegut's *Breakfast of Champions* (Delacorte Press, 1973), are probably the only ones who mourn this change as much as the school's alumni.

communicate is completely different than the proscribed use in the destination locale?

Controls on privacy are necessarily controls on communication: if I am not allowed to convey certain words/images/data because they might be used to identify an individual, then the authority that enforces these rules might deleteriously impinge on my communications in all the ways described here. Governmental regulation of privacy is rife with these troubling possibilities.

Does the "chilling effect" actually stifle communication/discussion, or is it just a theoretical concern discussed by Supreme Court judges and paranoiacs? Well, politicians in France experienced exactly what can happen when platform hosts are put in a position to be fearful of legal repercussions. In November 2019, France created new laws that require online content providers to track and publish information about any advertisers promoting political content through their platform. Instead of incurring the costs and expending the effort to comply with this law (and possibly infringing on the expressive rights of individuals, and violating laws in other countries), online communication platform Twitter chose to stop accepting all political advertising whatsoever. The French government was surprised to learn that its own advertising campaign on Twitter (to encourage voting in the next election) was discontinued as a direct result of this decision.[28] French politicians were likewise disappointed they will not be able to use that particular forum to run ads for their own elections.

They did not foresee the consequences. I am not sure how that's possible—the outcomes are immensely obvious to anyone, and lawmakers are supposedly in a better position to understand and anticipate outcomes for everyone under their influence. Even I can predict these types of outcomes . . . I live with the chilling effect, all the time.

For instance, there are some images I'd like to include in the next section of this book, but I am concerned those images might make the book illegal in certain markets. So, instead of being able to convey the information to you clearly, by showing you the images I'm talking about, I will refrain from doing so, which complicates communication and makes it more difficult to express myself. This is exactly the chilling effect, and it harms me (because I can't communicate as effectively as I might otherwise) and you (because you paid for information—this

---

[28] reason.com/2019/06/27/when-the-government-says-youre-fake-news

book—and the way the information might be conveyed to you has been needlessly complicated).

As for the cases of the comedians described earlier, Bruce prevailed in most, but not all of his cases. In some, a jury acquitted him; in others, charges were dropped or convictions overturned on appeal, but he was convicted in New York. Carlin's case was thrown out by a judge, who ruled that he had a right to say whatever words he chose, as long as the performance did not cause a public disturbance.

Power Outage

In a similar vein, regulation of communication in order to "protect" a group (or individuals) runs counter to any tradition of free thought, communication, or artistic expression. It also leads to a massive power disparity between the government and the citizens, where the government can dictate what the citizens might be allowed to say or do. This is as true for privacy-related data as it is for all other reasons that have been proffered for controlling information.

The first time I visited Germany, I was amazed to learn that a series of police raids had taken place while I was in the country, and people in 14 different German states had been arrested for words they had posted online.[29] Without exception, I personally found Germans to be extremely polite, informed, fairly reasonable, and welcoming; even when a German and I disagreed on a topic, we were able to discuss it without rancor or trouble. The wave of police action in response to printed words, therefore, seemed disconcerting and quite unlike the German attitudes and intellectualism I'd seen demonstrated.

These arrests were in response to a German law against "hate speech"—that is, inciting violence against a group of people of a specific ethnic or religious background. The online posts were largely part of a discussion among Germans who took an extreme dislike to the country's immigration policies and toward immigrants. What made the situation even more odd (from my perspective) was that the online posts were not public; the people in the conversation were part of (what they thought was) a private, secret social media group (but which had, in fact, been infiltrated by law enforcement agents). In my estimation, public calls

---

[29] www.thelocal.de/20160713/german-police-launch-first-nationwide-hate-speech-raids

to violence would be considered more dangerous, because they might reach a larger audience, than a close group of already likeminded people (where there is much less chance someone just wandered into a group full of people who hate a specific ethnicity/religion—it's hard to imagine someone *accidentally* clicked a link that is called "Jews Are Evil" or something similar).

Another aspect of this situation that intrigued me was part of the premise: discussion in a closed group, possibly involving incitement to violence but did not, itself, constitute conspiracy. I am very used to the American model of law enforcement, where criminals taking active steps to conduct a crime have already committed a crime (the "conspiracy" crime—you can be charged and prosecuted and punished for conspiring to do something, and law enforcement does not have to wait until you've conducted the crime in order to arrest and charge you). If a private, online group of people were actually discussing violent acts, to the point of planning to conduct those acts, I would expect (again, from an exclusively American vantage) that those people would be prosecuted for *that*, not for the supposed inherent danger of words on a screen. Instead, these people were arrested for words expressing dislike for people, but not necessarily conspiring to take specific violent actions.

The German constitution currently includes a prohibition against censorship; Germans are well aware of their own history and acknowledge the horror of governmental control of expression that comes from (or leads to) tyrannical dictatorships. They are dreadfully afraid and concerned about any potential future that includes the terrors of the past and have inculcated as much protection against that possibility as they could, in the very legal foundations of their nation.

With that said, for the same reasons, German criminal code has strict prohibitions against "symbols" of outlawed parties or organizations.[30] Presumably, the idea behind this law is that the lack of a unifying symbol would retard the efforts of hate groups to coalesce and conduct hateful activities and ultimately foil opportunities for re-creating past horrors. While the intent is certainly desirable (nobody sane wants a Fourth Reich), I think that depriving hateful people of certain symbols to prevent them from being hateful (or violent or terrible) is a level of optimism that beggars reality.

---

[30] germanlawarchive.iuscomp.org/?p=752#86

The original targets of the laws were those symbols associated with national socialism and communism; the laws have grown to take into account terrorist organizations as well. Unfortunately, there is no defined, exhaustive list of prohibited symbols, which has resulted in an extended absurdist game of artwork versus law enforcement: neo-Nazis will pick a symbol, the government will outlaw it, the neo-Nazis modify the symbol slightly, the government outlaws the new symbol, rinse and repeat. (Oddly, nobody involved seems to have the presence of mind or self-awareness to actually be clever or daring. If the prohibited groups just chose to pick a symbol so ubiquitous and innocuous that outlawing it would either be impossible or have a vast negative effect—say, Mickey Mouse ears—that would force the government to either arrest a lot of non-Nazis or admit that chasing cartoons is perhaps not the optimum way to counter detestable political movements.)

How does this pose a problem to humanity as a whole, if it only targets groups that the majority of humanity despises? First, the irony of a government stifling the expression of a loathed minority group should not be overlooked (especially when it's a German government)—that's pretty much exactly what the hated group would do if it took power and what German citizens are trying to prevent from occurring. More importantly, the action of the prohibition itself tends to have consequences that extend beyond what reasonable people would agree was the intent.

In 2005 and 2006, German authorities conducted operations to seize materials that featured anti-Nazi symbols, that is, symbols that depicted the swastika crossed out or a stick figure throwing a swastika in a trash can.[31] Police stormed the offices of a music production company and collected materials featuring such symbols. The 2017 video game *Wolfenstein II - The New Colossus*, set in an alternate world where Germany won World War II, included an image and the name of Adolf Hitler; the game makers were forced to modify the image to remove the character's mustache and rename him "Mr. Heiler" in order to sell the game to German customers.[32]

If you haven't already guessed, this is where I would have liked to include images depicting the outlawed symbols—the anti-Nazi symbols

---

[31] web.archive.org/web/20090113164205/www.tageblatt.de/main.cfm?DID=747071
[32] wolfenstein.fandom.com/wiki/Adolf_Hitler_(MachineGames)#Behind_the_scenes

that were cause for police action. But I'm not going to do so, because I'd like to be able to sell this book in Germany.

The German law prohibiting these symbols does, however, include an exception for using the symbols "to promote art or science, research or teaching, reporting about current historical events or similar purposes." This would theoretically avoid, for instance, the bizarre situation where a textbook that included historical photos of the people and locations involved in World War II would have to be edited and modified in such a way as to revise the historic record, leaving blank spots (and, evidently, removing facial hair) in the documents themselves.

But this begs the question and creates a risky situation: who, then, is the arbiter of what constitutes an artistic, scientific, or educational usage (never mind the "similar purposes," which is so vague I can't even imagine what that exception allows)? The answer is, of course, "the German government." But . . . isn't the law itself (and the German constitutional provision prohibiting censorship) intended to restrict the power of the German government, because that body had proven, historically, that such powers lead to abuse and tyranny?

Taking this a step further, what differentiates propaganda from art? I take the opportunity to point out that perhaps the single greatest producer of Nazi paraphernalia in the past 60 years has been Stephen Spielberg (between the Indiana Jones movies and the prequel TV show, episodes of *Amazing Stories*, *Schindler's List*, *Band of Brothers*, and *Saving Private Ryan*), and I don't for a minute believe Spielberg is in any way a Nazi sympathizer. But who, specifically, gets to choose which displays of swastikas are "art" and which are "propaganda"?[33] Is there a person who is uniquely qualified to determine whether a swastika featured in a film is artistic or whether it is a horrible affront to humanity? (Hint: if it were me, I would say the first three Indiana Jones movies were the former, while *Crystal Skull* is definitely the latter.)

And . . . does the way the product is received/perceived/portrayed somehow impact the determination of whether it is art? If I were to host a neo-Nazi support meeting and serve attendees popcorn while

---

[33] The Amazon Prime video series *The Man in the High Castle*, available for viewing in Germany, *does* feature many swastikas and even Adolf Hitler (with no name changes) as a prominent character. Moreover, oddly, the show has less literary and entertainment value than the video game that was forced to remove the symbols/name. But that's my opinion . . . and I'm not a government censor.

we all watched *Schindler's List* and I introduced and closed the film by portraying it as "a stirring depiction of the ill-fated efforts of heroic Aryans to conquer the insidious internal existential threat," would that, somehow, make the movie a piece of Nazi propaganda or in any way change the nature and quality of the film? Does the *intent* of the person who uses the symbols have, in any way, an effect on how the use of the symbol is qualified? *And do we want a government making this determination?* Does Steven Spielberg have to justify the creation as the creator, and should anyone want the artist to have to vindicate their own art? What about the role of the viewer—if you and I can partake in the same artwork and come to two very different conclusions/messages, is that the fault of the artist or an indictment of the work itself?

Seriously, would anyone want to watch a version of *The Sound of Music* where the Nazis had pixelated blurs on their arms and hats and cars where the swastikas would normally be?

Perhaps most crucially, what's the massive distinction between propaganda supporting the aims of a hated group and humanizing the people involved? Instead of Spielberg, I think of Wolfgang Petersen's seminal work, *Das Boot*: the film features a German submarine crew during World War II. The crew are not eager to commit genocide, they don't revere Hitler, and they don't seem motivated by hate or even politics; they are a team of dedicated Germans, at turns proud, fearful, bored, and angry—in a word, human.

While the typical viewer will probably not take from the experience a desire to create a Fourth Reich, the viewer may find themself sympathizing with the people involved, not wanting the characters to die. Honestly, I've seen the film more than once and can't even remember if any of the crew are members of the Nazi party or simply personnel in service to the German Navy, but that's the point: the audience is not being asked to support Nazism, but instead to perceive the horrors of war, a universal message, regardless of the point of view of the characters. At least, that's *my* take on the movie—should we allow a government tribunal to be the intermediary between us and the artist in order that we not be exposed to material the *government* has determined is unworthy?

Privacy laws convey this power, and more. If I am not allowed to even say the *name* of a politician I dislike because the name is "sensitive" information, or otherwise identify that person, how am I supposed to critique that person, their policies, or their politics? Once that power is ceded to a government, is there any reason at all to trust it won't be abused? That is, would a government/politician not want to stifle any dissent and criticism and therefore gladly use this power to remove any discussion that counters their own aims, in the name of "protecting privacy" (or for whatever reason the government/politician deems necessary)?

Governments/politicians may not be trustworthy when granted such powers, but they are dependable. We can depend on them to abuse the power they are granted. For example, from the moment Emmanuel Macron became president of France in 2017, he called loudly and strongly for restrictions on speech and expression, especially in electronic format, which he deemed disagreeable. Content Macron didn't like included incitement to violence, trolling, pornography, video games, harassment, political memes, and "deep fakes" (photos and video edited to change what they depict in a convincing way). But when Macron's bodyguard was caught on film posing as a police officer and viciously attacking demonstrators unprovoked, other Macron employees modified the footage of the incident and released the modified video to the public through anonymous, uncredited online accounts.[34] The modifications included splicing in video of violence unrelated to the actions captured in the original footage, to make it appear as if the behavior of the president's employee was, somehow, justifiable.

The hypocrisy is almost unbelievable—but not, quite, if you just always assume (as I do) that any power granted will, eventually, be power abused. And this wasn't done for the sake of protecting anyone other than the criminal in question and the criminal's employers: Macron and the government of France. It wasn't done in the name of public safety or to protect "the children" or the fate of the citizens of France. It was done for politics.

This is why I consider the German government's anti-expression efforts abhorrent, misguided, and ridiculous, but committed with benevolent intent—to deter or prevent would-be fascists—while I consider the French government's and in particular Macron and his staff's

[34] www.lemonde.fr/societe/article/2019/03/29/comment-l-elysee-a-fait-diffuser-un-montage-video-trompeur-pour-tenter-d-excuser-alexandre-benalla_5443397_3224.html

anti-expression efforts manipulative, self-serving, craven, small-minded, and downright evil.[35]

Top Cover

Government regulation, couched in whatever form of justification or excuse, can also lead to much greater abuses and increased chance of tyranny and despotism. This also might create situations that provide excuses/rationales for those who aid in the despots' efforts, allowing any single entity to claim, "well, it wasn't *my* fault, it was the *law*," as a means to offload culpability/accountability/responsibility.

Perhaps the starkest example is one that is also complicated and fraught with gray areas and supposition. Google (and its parent corporation, Alphabet, Inc.) is currently one of the largest technology companies in the world, in terms of market capitalization and market share (particularly in online advertising, operating systems for mobile devices, "Internet of Things" personal/residential devices, and online searches/ mapping/video hosting). China is one of the largest countries in the world, in terms of human population and land mass. Their relationship has been troubled from the get-go.

Google first started offering search engine services using Chinese language character sets in the year 2000, for global users. In 2006, Google created "google.cn," a search engine intended for use in mainland China; in accordance with Chinese law, Google agreed to only display

---

[35] And here's where the chilling effect gets really intriguing; discussion can also be stifled by means other than legislation. For instance, litigation (or even just the threat of it) can dampen conversation as well. In early drafts of this book, I included two additional sentences here; one sentence mentioned that the chilling effect cannot occur if the target does not fear the impact, and the other sentence stated my opinion that because I never expect or intend to sell books in France, I feel entirely safe insulting Macron, using a single-word term that metaphorically describes him as an [redacted]. A particularly vile [redacted]. The publisher of this book was not likewise comfortable in my use of this term (a stance that is probably quite reasonable, because if someone is going to get sued by Macron, it's probably going to be the publisher, not me, and the publisher is contractually obligated to legally defend the book). So . . . consider the book you're reading to be evidence of the success of the chilling effect. *[Nice try, Ben. We the editors do actually read the footnotes too! So readers, if you want to know what the author really thinks of a certain French politician, you'll need to listen to his podcast ("The Sensuous Sounds of INFOSEC," on* securityzed.com*) instead of reading it here. —Eds.]*

search results that are not prohibited by the Chinese government and the Communist Party (the driving political force in China). In effect, this censored Chinese expression (or, at least, was a form of censorship deployed against anyone trying to communicate with people inside China). For example, search requests for content disfavored by the Chinese government and Communist Party, such as photographic images from the Tiananmen Square demonstrations and massacre in 1989, would not return any relevant results.

To pause the historic review of the case for a moment, I'd like to discuss the ethics of this arrangement in order to juxtapose it against the situation that developed later.

I can see ethical arguments on both sides of Google's decision: on the one hand, Google is capitulating to force (an immoral force, at that) in adulterating search results, an action that tends to support a totalitarian regime by continuing the farce of information isolation and pretending that portions of history do not exist; on the other hand, *any* search results are more beneficial than *no* search results when people are engaged in online activity, so even a censored search platform offers some value to the people being oppressed (i.e., the citizens and residents of China). Agreeing to be an instrument of censorship is not the same as independently choosing to censor; Google did not initiate force against anyone and was facing a binary proposition (censor search results and get access to China, or don't censor results and don't get access). I don't think this arrangement could be said to have *caused* harm to anyone—lacking a credible and capable search engine is not a painful or deleterious condition (although many of my age cohort will agree: living in an age without any search engine, or an Internet altogether, sucked infinitely, compared to living with the Internet and search engines). Foregoing valid searches is not the same as, say, going without food, water, or oxygen.

However, the very fact that there are two sides of this arrangement to see kind of demonstrates the point of this section: Google was allowed to rationalize the choice ("support an immoral regime") and somewhat shield the action from criticism because Chinese law didn't really offer any option. The logical outcome to this line of thought is perhaps the one that's most disturbing: either all search technology vendors could have refused to offer service in China because censorship is immoral or the ones that did agree to censor results would be the sole providers in that region—that is, Google (and others) could hide behind the excuse, "well, *someone's* going to offer services, and that someone will censor results, so we might as well participate and censor results." This is an ugly defense, but totalitarian regimes create ugly choices. And the follow-up question would have to be: well, would Chinese citizens/residents be better off with *no* search engines, if all service providers refused to participate under immoral conditions? What serves the Chinese people best?

Again: ugly choices. But I can at least see why Google (or any provider) might go with either option.

It does seem like Google itself, as a corporate entity, was chafing with the problems arising from this arrangement, too, as we continue the case history: in 2010, Google announced that it would no longer be willing to censor search results and would completely eliminate its search services in China, if the censorship requirement continued. (Before giving unearned moral credit to Google for this high-minded choice, this decision was at least partly in response to hacking attempts staged by the Chinese military and entities associated with the Chinese government against Google and other tech companies the year prior.[36])

Then Google redirected all searches launched from the mainland China Google address (google.cn) to the Google address/search engine in Hong Kong (google.com.hk). While Hong Kong became part of China in 1997, some of China's laws (such as the ban of prohibited material in Internet search results) do not apply to Hong Kong. Search results via Google's Hong Kong service were not censored.

Predictably, the Chinese government then shut down Internet access to all Google search engines a few weeks later. This ban lasted only a short time, but Google ended its practice of redirecting searches through Hong Kong (and therefore offering uncensored search results) a few weeks after that.

The situation continued to fluctuate until 2014, by which point Google search and email services were no longer available in mainland China. I am uncertain as to whether this happened because the Chinese government blocked Google or Google decided to stop offering these services in the region. There are claims that Google's services have been blocked by a Chinese government program known colloquially as "The Great Firewall."[37] Conversely, Google's leadership seemed to claim

---

[36] www.reuters.com/article/us-google-hacking-idUSTRE7506U320110602
[37] www.cnn.com/2018/10/01/tech/google-china-censorship/index.html

that it had been the company's choice to refrain from participating in China, as part of a moral stance.[38] Which possibility is most accurate is not important. What's important is what happened next.

In 2016, Google commenced plans to return services to mainland China. This included negotiations with the Chinese government and Communist Party, as to what concessions Google would have to make to get official permission to operate there. In August 2018, Google announced plans for its new Chinese search engine, dubbed Dragonfly.

In September 2018, online news source The Intercept published a report claiming that an internal Google memo outlined a number of disconcerting aspects of the Dragonfly program. These included a capability to capture the geographic position of users, as well as collecting a record of their browsing history. Moreover, sources within Google told The Intercept that a Chinese entity would be granted unfettered access to Dragonfly's database.[39]

So what? Isn't this pretty much what all modern Internet users have come to expect and what we already know—that we get the service in exchange for handing our data to the entity providing the service . . . and that none of our online activity is private because we've knowingly made that exchange? Yes, to a large degree: we know that we are sharing some information about our activity and ourselves with the service provider. In many cases, the service wouldn't work unless the provider knew something (for instance, a search engine can't work unless it knows what you want to search for—the search term you give it; of course, how long the provider *keeps* that data after the transaction is complete, and what it does with that data, is something we rarely consider). We know that online providers often share the data they gather with advertisers; it's how the provider finances the service without having to charge a monetary cost instead. So why would sharing the information with any entity, such as a Chinese government agency or contractor, be any more troublesome?

Chinese law prohibits its citizens from engaging in a wide variety of activities that much of the modern world considers human rights: having children,[40] speaking out against the government or the Communist

---

[38] Google's then-CEO was quoted as saying, "In a long enough time period, do I think that this kind of regime approach [to censorship] will end? I think absolutely." www.technologyreview.com/2018/12/19/138307/how-google-took-on-china-and-lost

[39] The Intercept has kept a full record of its coverage of Google and the Dragonfly program specifically, theintercept.com/collections/google-dragonfly-china

[40] www.china.org.cn/e-white/familypanning

Party,[41] and even choosing your own religion.[42] Other human behavior, while not illegal, may be subject to censorship and extralegal persecution, such as LGBT identification, expression, and association.[43] Punishment for these activities is often swift and brutal and have included arrests, incarceration/internment, forced medical procedures/surgeries, and even murder. Since 2013, China has created a program of forcing more than a million people into concentration camps, forcing them to perform slave labor, and enduring propagandistic "re-education" indoctrination, because these people had committed the crime of . . . having the wrong religion and ethnicity.[44]

Any company providing information to the Chinese government that might lead to such consequences is party to these outrages, and there is no way to limit ethical and moral culpability—nobody can claim, "well, I didn't arrest/incarcerate/mutilate/murder anyone; I just shared some data about them with the government/Party, and the government/Party did those things." A privacy law that constrains the government from collecting such information would have to be founded on the premise that the government intends to allow itself to be constrained . . . and that a government that does not recognize basic human rights will somehow just merrily comply with a law telling it not to detect the people it is targeting.

After a few public denials about the nature, scope, and characteristics of Dragonfly from Google leadership, the project was shut down in December 2018, ostensibly because of massive dissent within and among the teams of engineers tasked with building it.

In 2009, Google provided almost a third of all Internet search services in China.[45] Today, search services in China are largely provided by Chinese tech companies. While writing this, I tried to search "Tank Man," via google.cn, and it redirected me to google.com.hk. After that initial search, all my attempted connections to google.cn were

---

[41] www.history.com/topics/china/tiananmen-square

[42] web.archive.org/web/20160417122423/freedomhouse.org/sites/default/files/12222014_FH_ChinaReport2014_FINAL.pdf

[43] www.thelancet.com/journals/lanpub/article/PIIS2468-2667(19)30153-7/fulltext

[44] www.aljazeera.com/indepth/opinion/china-holds-million-uighur-muslims-concentration-camps-180912105738481.html

[45] www.technologyreview.com/2018/12/19/138307/how-google-took-on-china-and-lost

immediately redirected to google.com.hk. (Tank Man is the worldwide nickname for the heroic Chinese man who faced down approaching tanks during the Tiananmen Square massacre. The iconic photo is famous around the world and can be instantly found by searching for "Tank Man" on the Internet . . . unless you are in China.)

This is just one case of how bad regulation creates the potential, motivation, and situation for companies to make bad choices that could lead to very bad things. I am not singling Google out as the sole company to ever cooperate with governments to the detriment of individuals (and, in fact, it seems that it was action on the part of individuals within Google that changed the company's course for the better). But this is what happens when power is granted to a central authority. It's also worth remembering that, from the perspective of the Chinese government and Communist Party, *this regulation is in place to protect China and Chinese citizens.*

The government and Party view the situation this way: if citizens could get access to some kinds of information (about opposition political parties, unapproved religions, LGBT activism groups, historic counter-Party demonstrations, etc.), the citizens might be disenchanted with the government and the Party, and work to change the status quo; because the government and Party are the very best way to manage China (according to the government and Party), and disenchantment/change is disruptive, that disruption would ultimately harm the Chinese people.

No villain sees themselves as villainous; they actually believe they are acting in furtherance of the best interest of "the people." This is true whether you're a politician, Party member, or James Bond antagonist.

Coincidentally, it was around this period when Alphabet changed its corporate motto from "Don't Be Evil" to "Do the Right Thing."

The Right Thing sometimes includes ignoring a chilling effect, or foregoing potential profit from a market because trying to profit there would preclude acting in an ethical and moral manner. For instance, I know including this section in this book will get my book banned from China; I will not be allowed to sell a single copy to one-seventh of the world's population. Moreover, this may result in my other books, already translated into Chinese, also being banned. But not including the Chinese situation in a book about the current state of global privacy would be Doing the Wrong Thing.

Now You See It . . .

Legislation and administrative law are not the only possible forms of governmental regulation, of course. There is also the potential for regulation through judicial action. A court can issue a gag order or a cease-and-desist order or seal records or otherwise mandate the secrecy of proceedings or communications. If other forms of regulation aren't sufficient for the purpose and prone to abuse, surely this is an optimum way to ensure privacy?

Except that trying to hide something often calls attention to that very thing.

On the Internet, this is called the Streisand Effect, named for the singer/actress who tried to sue a photographer and various organizations and online vendors for posting a photograph of her home online.[46] Streisand claimed the photo "invade[d] her privacy, violate[d] the 'anti-paparazzi' statute, [sought] to profit from her name, and threaten[ed] her security."[47] She asked for millions of dollars in damages (what possible damage she incurred, I am totally unclear). Prior to her lawsuit, the photo had only been viewed six times (two of those downloads were by attorneys working for Streisand); the month following the filing of the suit, it was accessed 420,000 times.

> **NOTE**   Unlike the chilling effect keeping me from including swastikas earlier in the book, I am not including the photo here because I respect the property rights of the photographer and the organization that owns the photo; instead, I will include a link: www.californiacoastline.org/cgi-bin/image.cgi?image=3850&mode=sequential&flags=0. The photographer and the organizations involved countersued Streisand under California's law to prevent abuse of the court system to stifle expression, and Streisand was forced to pay more than $177,000 in damages.[48]

In psychology, the desire to know something that someone is trying to hide is often linked to "reactance"—the impetus to respond to an

[46] www.techdirt.com/articles/20030624/1231228.shtml and www.techdirt.com/articles/20050105/0132239.shtml
[47] www.californiacoastline.org/streisand/lawsuit.html
[48] arquivo.pt/wayback/20090706034700 and www.mindfully.org/Reform/2003/Barbra-Streisand-Coastal3dec03.htm

attempt to stifle or subjugate you, perceived as an attempt to limit your freedoms. In military and espionage circles, the efforts to hide unclassified indicators of secretive activities are called *operational security* or OPSEC. OPSEC actions are extremely complicated, because the effort to hide something can become an indicator of that thing or draw attention to it. (One apocryphal tale reprinted in many sources describes how a large number of pizza delivery orders indicated the launch of offensive operations during the first Gulf War in 1991; while the veracity of this is questionable, the US Army took it seriously enough to change OPSEC rules.[49])

Currently, many courts will try to protect privacy through any number of means, for a variety of reasons. Most of these efforts are purportedly to protect persons involved with a given case, to include victims, victims' families, and witnesses, more so when the persons involved are minors. This does lead to some very bizarre situations, such as when evidence of multiple crimes was withheld from open viewing in a Canadian court, supposedly to protect the victims' families, but which also was perceived as diminishing the culpability of another of the perpetrators, who had been given qualified immunity in return for cooperation with the prosecutors. The prosecution, allegedly, did not realize the full extent of one of the perpetrators' involvement in the crimes and (supposedly) would not have agreed to the negotiated sentence if they had; the videotapes showed how wrong the prosecution had been, and the court's decision to withhold that evidence from the public was largely perceived as an attempt to protect the authorities from the political and professional consequences of their bad decision, not the victims or survivors.[50]

Another aspect of this secrecy is that it seems unevenly applied, both in terms of content and subjects. Maintaining privacy through having a judge sealing a record that would otherwise be public seems to be the exclusive province of people who are rich and powerful and have the wherewithal to bring legal expertise to the domain of the court. This can create some oddly dichotomous situations, such as when a porn star sued her ex-husband but had a judge seal the record; everything

---

[49] www.army.mil/article/2758/army_releases_new_opsec_regulation
[50] www.thecanadianencyclopedia.ca/en/article/homolkas-plea-bargain-revealed

about the litigants' lives would otherwise seem to be in the public view, but *that* case somehow contained something worth keeping private.[51]

As a pure example of the aforementioned reactance factor, this begs the question, "for what possible reason would the court seal the data?" It draws more attention than it might have, had it just been a public record, and it demonstrates that people with money may be treated differently by the courts than those without it. In a democratic, egalitarian society, this would not be the case. Moreover, this practice (at least in the jurisdiction used in the example) blunts the ability of the citizens to find recourse, as even the name of the judge who ordered the record sealed is shrouded in secrecy—there is little means to hold someone accountable/responsible for this decision.

The Government Would Never Lie to Its Overseers, Right?

The following is an excerpt from testimony given by James Clapper, the Director of National Intelligence, before the US Senate on March 12, 2013[52]:

> Senator Wyden: . . . does the NSA collect any type of data at all on millions, or hundreds of millions, of Americans?
>
> Director Clapper: No, sir.
>
> Senator Wyden: It does not?
>
> Director Clapper: Not wittingly.

Riiiiiiight.[53]

Stressing It

To recap and restate, industry experts, politicians, and activists want to protect the public. The perceived threat is monolithic, ultra-powerful

[51] Geary, Frank. "Porn star bares all except lawsuit against ex," *Las Vegas Review-Journal*, February 14, 2007.
[52] www.youtube.com/watch?v=QwiUVUJmGjs
[53] www.history.com/this-day-in-history/edward-snowden-discloses-u-s-government-operations

tech giants that capture all our data. The proposed solution is granting more power to centralized authorities, especially governments. Because no single person could protect themselves from the forces currently arrayed against each of us. I get it. I see the promise of comfort in that mechanism, and the desire for an instrument that will impose account-ability on the industry as a whole and level the scales such that individ-uals are not crushed by behemoths. I respect the intent, most certainly. To be frank, I am just as concerned and scared of what our lives (and my life, in particular) will be like when all shreds of privacy are gone, and I am totally exposed. I am not eager to see the post-private world . . . but I know it's coming. And it's coming soon enough that I will probably have to live in that world.

But I can say, with all certainty, that governmental regulation is not the panacea its proponents hope for. If anything, it will bring more horrors than the loss of privacy will and will only serve to retard the inevitable transparency that will expose everyone and everything. That will occur regardless, and trying to delay it through the use of statute, mandate, administrative function, or judicial intervention will only exacerbate any problems with the transition, and create more, newer ones.

There's a final, more dreadful possibility, too, and I want to make clear that I'm not pointing the finger at any particular person or group with this statement; I am saying this in the general sense. If anyone chooses to move ahead with parliamentary activity even in the face of and knowledge that unintended consequences will occur *but wants to regulate something anyway*, then . . . can we really say that those con-sequences were unintended by that person? I say this because I cannot believe, or am not willing to give the benefit of the doubt to lawmakers and other advocacy entities, that these people—smart, educated, adult, informed, capable—can have any grasp on history whatsoever and not realize that every law, every regulation, has downstream effects beyond the stated intent and that every power granted to government has been and will be abused at some point, to some extent, often in dramatic and terrible ways.

You can't call it a "backfire" or "mistake" or "accident" if you know it's a direct effect of your action, and I'm saying, right here, that giving a central authority the right to regulate data, in the hope of obtaining "privacy," is a forlorn hope and will only lead to abuses by that authority and greater disparity between powerful entities and individuals.

7

A Good Solution: Ubiquity of Access

"See me . . . hear me . . . feel me."

– *Roger Daltrey, Tommy*

The premise, again: privacy is going away. It might go slowly, especially if we take steps to retard its loss; it might go quickly, in just a few years. The loss of privacy will cause enormous damage, as the transition will unveil many things about ourselves to each other (well, actually, it will reveal everything about ourselves). If we act to slow the dissolution of privacy, we're going to cause more damage than the conversion would otherwise include. (See: all the previous chapters, especially Chapter 6.)

I don't mean for this to sound bleak, or hopeless. In fact, I'd like to add a new flavor to the current prevailing conversation regarding the subject—anticipating a post-private world and realizing what it might have to offer. There are numerous benefits we can reap from a world without privacy, and I'm going to explore some of them in this chapter, as well as some (nontechnical) suggestions as to how we might accomplish them.

The nice thing is that we're already recognizing some of the positive benefits we get from trading privacy for value. Many online services are financed with the value of our data instead of money we'd otherwise be charged, which saves each of us the cash. This isn't actually a new model, either, that just occurred in the past few years; this is how newspapers, magazines, radio, television, and other media were financed for more than 100 years—the subscription/cover price wasn't the revenue that made those businesses profitable, it was the ability to track readers/ viewers and sell access to those audiences to advertisers.

Moreover, with our willingness to part with our data, we've increased our own individual reach: if I'm willing to put my name/likeness/

preferences/capabilities/desires out into the public arena, I may get more customers, romantic partners, colleagues, opportunities, and friends than if I lock myself in my home or limit my interactions to the people on the neighboring farm or just within my own city. Using current technology, I have instant, global reach to markets and people . . . if I'm willing to expose myself, to more or less extent.

And, in addition to both those benefits, we've also recognized in society that decreased privacy leads to enhanced efficiency and convenience. If I am willing to part with identifying information, I can shop online, conduct business transactions remotely, and generally take part in a world far beyond what I would be limited to if I had to engage solely face-to-face with other parties.

These are simple examples that we're all already familiar with. But I'd like to suggest a few others that might not be so common and expound on how those might be utilized in ways that might not be already obvious.

If Everybody Knows Everything, Nobody Has an Advantage

Information has value. Some information has more value; often, the quality of data that makes it precious is scarcity/limitation of access. This is not always the case: some information has value regardless how many people know it—knowing the weather forecast, how to perform a basic task, the text of a Mark Twain essay; the value of these things is not diminished with popularity/ubiquity. Libraries are based on this principle, as is advertising, news media, and the idea that a populace can choose its own public servants via election. Some colleges and universities are even making their courses available free of charge, online.[1]

More importantly, the free availability of many types of information doesn't cause anyone any harm: if you know how to cook a meal or do math or how to drive a car, this does not have any detrimental effect on me whatsoever.

In some cases, the more information and knowledge everyone has, the *better* life is for everyone else. Literacy is one example, likewise broad access to childhood education. The information that explains how

---

[1] ocw.mit.edu/index.htm

to provide first aid or cardiopulmonary resuscitation or the Heimlich maneuver is actually more beneficial the more people know it. Honestly, I would feel much more comfortable riding in a commercial jetliner if everyone aboard knew how to fly it, instead of only two or three. We aren't trying to keep the Pythagorean theorem or Newton's laws or the scientific method secret from anyone; those are data that have significant value, and that value only increases with wide dissemination. The more people who know how to grow, harvest, and store their own crops, safely handle a firearm, perform rescue swimming, physically defend themselves, construct a rhetorical argument with logic, or convey ideas and meaning through personal expression, the better.

However, the value of some data rests in the limitation of access to or knowledge of that data. The knowledge of how to make meatloaf isn't particularly valuable, but *my* recipe for meatloaf might have value, if I'm a chef and my meatloaf is somehow better than everyone else's.[2] A company might have a list of customers that is valuable . . . but only to advertisers or other companies in that same industry that want to reach the same audience. The entire concept of "insider trading" is that the workers/leaders of a company have access to knowledge that the ostensible owners (the investors and shareholders, or the public who can become shareholders) and customers do not also have; the limitation of access is what makes the data more valuable.

If we imagine a world where all the information is known to everyone, then the disparity of value is neutralized. Yes, some aspects of our lives will be diminished; trade secrets and the inner workings of certain business functions (a list of customers, for example) will become bereft of value. This does not eliminate competition (and the benefits to customers/the public resulting from competition), because secrecy is not the only competitive edge—companies can also compete on the skill/training of the workforce, talent, diligence, quality, price, delivery, etc. There may be some businesses that rely on controlled dissemination of information (this one, for instance: this book is available for sale to the public, but it is not freely available to the public), but that can be addressed in other ways, which I'll get to a bit further in this chapter.

---

[2] This is purely a hypothetical example. I am completely unable to make meatloaf altogether.

Atomicity, Again

Then there are other kinds of information that have inherent value, but only when the information can be acted on. For instance, data about human anatomy and physiology is not being kept secret: you can learn absolutely anything you want about how the human body functions. However, reading every book about every facet of biology does not make you a surgeon. Practicing medicine takes more than data—it requires instruction, repetition, practical experience, and innate physical acumen.

This is why one of the threats a post-private world entails (public knowledge of destructive information) is not necessarily as risky as we might suppose. For instance, we may fear that the knowledge of how to make atomic, biological, or chemical weapons might become known publicly . . . but it already is. That information is widely available.[3] It's not the *data* that is valuable/dangerous . . . it's people acting on the data. And, at the moment, acquiring the elements of a useful weapon of mass destruction, assembling them safely (safely, that is, for the weapon maker), and deploying them are the difficult aspects.

The key words in the previous sentence are *at the moment*—soon, it will become child's play for anyone to make a weapon that can kill everyone. 3D printers and home genetics labs lead to a situation where anyone with access to data (in the form of recipes/templates/DNA strings) will be able to cheaply and easily create products that can kill hundreds, thousands, or perhaps millions of people.[4] It is tempting to suggest that we will still need privacy/secrecy to prevent that information from becoming widely available, but this is simply not feasible. The genie is out of the bottle already; any effort to recover that data from public view and make it secret again is not only pointless, but would cause unimaginable damage and harm in the trying.

---

[3] Here, I'll make it even more widely available: to make a nuclear weapon, you take enough fissile material (typically enriched uranium or plutonium) to achieve critical mass and push it all together very quickly (usually by shaping it like a soccer ball and surrounding it with conventional explosive, all of which is triggered at the same time)—bang, you've got an atomic explosion. To make chlorine gas, mix bleach and ammonia. To make a biological weapon, have a child.

[4] Ronald Bailey. "I made antibiotic-resistant E. coli in my kitchen, and the world didn't end." reason.com/2018/05/31/adventures-in-home-biohacking

It might be better for us, as a species, to start wondering what it will be like when broody teenagers consider externalizing their ennui instead of directing it at themselves in the form of suicide/self-harm. If Eric Harris and Dylan Klebold had access to a customized strain of vaccine-resistant smallpox, might they have used it on Columbine High School instead of firearms and improvised explosives?

Attempts along these lines have already been made by amateur (non-nation-state) groups: the Rajneeshee religious group used salmonella to poison more than 750 people in Washington State,[5] and the Aum Shinrikyo religious group used sarin gas in an attack on the Tokyo subway system, killing 13 and affecting almost 1,000 others.[6]

Even with access to the data *and* the ease of creation, deployment still seems to pose a major hurdle for amateurs attempting to conduct mass murder.[7] There is something else that might help reduce the risk, though: an end to privacy.

An End to Crime?

Without privacy, none of these groups/criminals would have been able to prepare their attacks, much less execute them. And, oddly, they would probably not have had the motivation to harm anyone, but let me address that a little later in this section.

A surveillance state is frightening—it seems to offer the worst of all dystopian qualities: you are constantly under observation, and, at any time, you might get snatched up by the authorities, who have ready-made evidence (the recordings of your crime) with which to prosecute and sentence you. This is the existential horror that loss of privacy holds for many people. I definitely number myself among that group; all the features of an all-seeing state from every bit of literature that even touches on the subject are utterly terrible.

NOTE   Popular culture runs rampant with references to the trope of power malfeasance linked to loss of privacy. George Orwell's *1984*,

---

[5] www.cdc.gov/phlp/docs/forensic_epidemiology/Additional%20Materials/Articles/Torok%20et%20al.pdf
[6] www.japantimes.co.jp/news/2020/03/25/national/25-years-tokyo-attack-aum-shinrikyo/#.XyzDfn5OnRQ
[7] www.ncbi.nlm.nih.gov/books/NBK233494/#ddd00091

Secker & Warburg, (1949), is perhaps the best-known depiction of a dystopia that includes a massive surveillance state. Other popular media portrayals of the danger of the loss of privacy include Solzhenitsyn's works (both fiction and nonfiction), the haunting masterpiece *The Conversation*, and the later action vehicle that nods to Gene Hackman's character from that film, *Enemy of the State*. Taking it a step further, *The Hunger Games* series included the idea that even someone's violent death might be used for both entertainment purposes and to prop up a repressive regime (notions echoed in other works as well, including Stephen King's novella *The Running Man* and the Schwarzenegger film very loosely based on it, as well as Roger Corman's *Death Race 2000*). Even the Beatles included a line referring to pervasive Soviet surveillance in their "Back in the USSR": "honey, disconnect the phone" (as the Soviet spy apparatus was known to use the mouthpieces of phones inside citizens' homes as microphones to listen in on conversations). We have an extremely well-documented aversion to any situation where someone is constantly looking over our shoulder.

For just a moment, I ask you to consider, however, what truly total transparency would mean from a criminal perspective, other than the dread of impending arrest and prosecution. If all actions and speech of all people, everywhere, were recorded and stored, with simple recall capability (such that anyone's deeds or words from any specific point in time/location could be reviewed, instantly), would that act as a uniform deterrent to most crime? If the soon-to-be-criminal knew, before committing the crime, that everything they said and did could be reviewed afterward, would they still perform the illegal act?

I think there may be some deterrent value: we tend to behave differently, in a quasi-private world, when we believe we're under observation and will be held accountable for our actions. Speeding traffic slows when there is a police car present. Students are on their best behavior when their parent is in the classroom. Everyone behaves in a manner other than normal (for good or ill) when there's a camera in front of their face.

NOTE Obviously, some crime will still exist in a transparent, post-private world. Crimes of passion or desperation come to mind.

There are several fatal flaws in the current surveillance model that makes it unviable as a deterrent to crime. These include people's lack of awareness of just how little privacy they still have, limited data storage and monitoring capabilities, and the fact that surveillance data is available only to specific entities instead of everyone.

First Fatal Flaw

Does the current model, where surveillance/detection/monitoring is imperfect and limited to specific groups/agencies, prevent crime? Not at all—I was shocked when I read a claim, many years ago, that London has three security cameras for every person in the city. This claim seems far from correct, but it captured my interest. (It seems more likely that there is one security camera for every 5–15 people in London, but these numbers are incredibly difficult to capture, because of the wide variety of privately owned systems, and lack of good survey methods.[8][9]) London is far from a crime-free city; 149 people were murdered there in 2019,[10] and the crime rate in general seems to be increasing over the past seven years.[11] (Again, much like the topic of suicide discussed earlier in the book, measuring "crime" is tricky, because of all ways data collection/analysis can be affected by externalities and incentives.)

If knowing you're being observed affects behavior, and the most-watched cities in the world are not crime-free, why doesn't the current model work?

I think the paramount (but not the only) reason surveillance doesn't work right now is that people have not yet realized just how thoroughly they're being observed; the idea hasn't sunk in yet. Right now, people who commit a crime do so because they have the belief that they can get away with it. People don't *feel* like all crimes will be logged and evidence against them instantly recorded. I violate traffic laws all the time, with fairly high confidence I will only occasionally be caught and punished.

This belief is aided by law enforcement efforts to downplay the amount and depth of intrusive surveillance capability that already

---

[8] www.precisesecurity.com/articles/Top-10-Countries-by-Number-of-CCTV-Camerasweb.archive.org/web/20150923185058
[9] www.bigbrotherwatch.org.uk/files/priceofprivacy/Price_of_privacy_2012.pdf
[10] www.thesun.co.uk/news/10675945/london-stabbings-2020-murders-knife-crime-statistics
[11] www.statista.com/statistics/380963/london-crime-rate

exists.[12] [13] [14] Right now, the authorities don't want citizens to know just how much information is constantly being collected and how little privacy remains. The illusion of privacy does not discourage people from criminal acts.

It's only a matter of time, however, before the true lack of privacy becomes apparent, and people realize that there's very little they can do to obscure their behavior from observation. My guess is that this will happen not because of law enforcement action but from private citizens acting in their own interest; security monitoring capability has become so cheap and easy to use, just about anyone can acquire and set up a surveillance system for their home, workplace, or car. We've already had more than a decade of crimes being captured via "nanny cams" deployed by homeowners.[15] Similarly, bicyclists and joggers wear cameras to deter muggings and hit-and-run accidents (or at least to help identify and hold accountable the perpetrators). Law enforcement might want to hide their abilities to monitor citizens, but citizens want the deterrent effect constant monitoring provides. The diminishment of privacy is going to increase as observation and surveillance continually grows.

Other Fatal Flaws

Right now, the reason people aren't behaving as if they're under constant surveillance is because they are not under constant surveillance. This is not because the technology does not exist to capture everyone's location/activity/conversations—it most certainly does. But there are two limitations on this data, which keep the information from being used successfully as evidence/deterrent: storage and monitoring ability.

Data storage technology is constantly expanding, but there is a still a cost and maximum capacity associated with retention of information.

---

[12] www.eff.org/deeplinks/2013/01/what-fbi-doesnt-want-you-know-about-its-surveillance-techniques

[13] www.seattlepi.com/local/crime/article/Feds-sue-Seattle-to-keep-FBI-surveillance-camera-8107443.php

[14] reason.com/2019/04/24/the-feds-are-dropping-child-porn-cases-instead-of-revealing-info-on-their-surveillance-systems

[15] There are too many references to actual incidents to cite any specific one here as a general case. Also, to make your own research activities more effective when trying to find security-pertinent information, be sure to enable Safe Search options on your web browser when using search strings that include "caught on nanny cam."

We generally don't capture *everything*, because there's nowhere to put it (or, at least, keeping it all would be cost-prohibitive).

Monitoring is the other issue: for everyone to be watched all the time, you'd need every person to be constantly viewing at least one other person . . . and then we can extrapolate the ridiculousness of the situation from there. Instead, data that features criminal activity must almost necessarily be used ex post facto; we call up the recording of what occurred after the crime has happened in order to punish the wrongdoer(s).

The combination of these two limitations highlights the shortcoming of each: *finding* the appropriate data that showcases the crime can be difficult and only becomes more difficult the more data you capture. Instead of just having to search for a needle in a haystack, you have to search for a needle in a million haystacks. In the INFOSEC field, the problem of log review/analysis is addressed by setting a *clipping level*, that is, choosing the granularity and specificity of the data you're capturing to reasonably find what you want to locate later. There are also products that enhance real-time search and automated analysis to augment monitoring performed by human analysts (that is, humans who are analyzing data, not necessarily the analysis of humans).

So we don't, as a species, have uniform, ubiquitous, real-time monitoring quite yet, largely because of limitations on data storage and reasonable data analysis. I predict these limits will evaporate pretty quickly, simply because the demand for more (storage and analysis tools, both) is driving bigger, better, faster technologies.

I am not personally encouraging this development, where we transition from privacy to no privacy. I'm not even looking forward to it. But I recognize it and want to begin the conversation that we *should* be having ("how are we going to deal with this, and how best can we optimize that world?") instead of the one we *are* having ("how do we stop this?").

Final Fatal Flaw

There's one more aspect of the current model that makes it unviable as a deterrent: right now, broad surveillance data is collected and used by limited entities (typically, governments and law enforcement agencies), instead of being universally available to everyone.

Governments/law enforcement entities have several reasons for limiting access to information, and particularly information related to criminal activity: concerns for personal safety of the data subject, perverse incentives, and statutory compliance, among others. Under the current model, all these reasons for limiting access to personal data create a dichotomy of power: governments/law enforcement agencies have more than the citizens they serve.

However, the ubiquity of access to recording devices *and* broadcast/sharing of data is already greatly diminishing the power disparity. The recent wave of videos featuring malfeasance by police (from both mobile devices owned by private citizens and police bodycams/dashcams) are quickly leveling the field between police and policed. This can only continue as privacy erodes, until honesty in enforcement is all that remains. I think we can all look forward to that—even the police, who will benefit from vindication against false accusations, in addition to the ease with which they'll be able to identify and capture lawbreakers.

Is there a flipside to this opportunity? Will lawbreakers also be able to monitor police and avoid capture? Of course. This is a seesaw that has been rocking back and forth between enforcers and criminals forever. From an IT perspective, in just the past 50 years, would-be lawbreakers have used technologies such as police-band radio monitors, radar detectors, and camera-obscuring lasers to try to anticipate and deter detection and arrest, among other techniques. With the loss of privacy, criminals will know the location of police and will use this to attempt to avoid capture.

But . . . to what end? When everyone knows who performed which crime(s), running away from the authorities is a bit pointless. When there's no refuge, no means to blend back into the law-abiding society, how does avoiding arrest and punishment really serve the criminal in any way? Again, on a macro level, the loss of privacy might seem a detriment but will actually function well.

An End to the *Need* for Crime?

When I mentioned the crimes involving chem/bio weapons earlier in this chapter, I also mentioned that not only might crime be deterred, but also detected prior to commission (in the preparation/planning phase), and that the purpose for the specific crimes listed might not exist. Let me expound on that a bit.

Both the Rajneeshee and Aum Shinrikyo attacks were the result of the leaders of those groups reacting to what they perceived as existential attacks, mainly because they feared immediate loss of secrecy. (This is also true of another infamous mass murder using chemical weapons, the Jonestown massacre, in which more than 900 members of a religious group drank [or were forced to drink] poison; the group's leader, Reverend Jim Jones, was afraid that the true condition of the group would imminently be exposed to the public, including authorities and members' families.[16])

To state it clearly, I am not, in any way, vindicating, excusing, or justifying the actions of these groups or the decisions made by their leaders. Those choices and acts were pure evil. So how does a lack of privacy lead to a better, nonevil result?

The leaders of those groups, to a greater or lesser degree, feared exposure of the inner workings of their respective groups, which would likely lead to the leaders' loss of power/privilege. Only through privacy did those leaders obtain power . . . because, in each case, their power was only acquired through deception and/or hypocrisy. If the *members* of those groups, as well as everyone else in the world, knew the full scope of their leaders' communications and activities (including knowledge of the leaders' financial transactions), those leaders might not have acquired nearly the level of power they each had and, therefore, would not have had as much to lose (nor the wherewithal to carry out their deadly operations).

To reiterate, those leaders feared exposure; if there's nothing to expose, there's no fear, and without fear there is no need to resort to violence.

Of course, those people, the evil leaders of the groups, were insane. And I'm trying to apply rational thought processes to crazy people, which just won't work. So, crimes involving purely crazed behavior cannot be deterred (or pre-emptively detected, in most cases) by total transparency.

That said, it is worth questioning whether the insanity of the leaders of those groups was exacerbated by the eventual power they acquired; if they had just been insane and not been able to use deception and privacy to snow their adherents, would they have eventually ever been in the position to attack anyone, and would they have even felt the need to do so?

---

[16] jonestown.sdsu.edu

A regular crazy person is largely ignored by other people, but when a crazy person receives adoration and sustenance from a large group, that can fuel potential megalomaniacal and paranoid tendencies. Such a leader, emboldened, is apt to strike out at any danger to their power base, real or imagined. But if there was an end to privacy, where a regular crazy person can readily be identified and ignored, that might limit the number of crazy people who build such a following that they opt for mass murder.

Of course, mass murder is not the only crime that privacy feeds into.

Blackmail, for instance, can happen only in a quasi-private world; the target wants something kept private (perhaps, say, evidence of a previous activity the target engaged in, such as wearing a culturally-insensitive Halloween costume, or the commission of a crime), and the blackmailer threatens to expose the shameful/criminal activity unless the target pays the blackmailer. The entire concept of the crime hinges on the fact that the target *wants to keep something hidden*; if the entirety of everyone's actions were already known, there would be no leverage for the blackmailer to exploit.

Privacy is also necessary for fraud and deception; if all parties to a transaction are fully aware of all information bearing on it, then nobody is at a disadvantage, and no party can take value from another illicitly. The entire concept of "insider trading" is based on the premise that some people will have access to information that others do not, putting the first group into a position where they can disproportionately profit from the situation in a way that the second group could not. Circumstances allowing for this type of chicanery could not exist without inequities of information access. And there would be no need for secrecy in business if all other forms of privacy and secrecy were eliminated: if true ownership of all assets, be them tangible or intellectual property, is transparent, there is no concern for theft.

This doesn't eliminate potential for what a third party, someone not participating in the transaction, might consider an inequitable trade: if you think I am stupid for spending a million dollars for a shiny rock, you are welcome to that opinion, and I am still able to make that choice, but at no point will I be unaware of any information regarding that rock, including any assertions made in marketing that rock ("this rock is precious"/I know exactly how many other, similar rocks there are available for sale; "this rock cures gout,"/I know exactly how many other people have been previously cured of gout by this rock; "this rock will make another person love you,"/I know exactly how many people this rock has caused to fall in love before, etc.). I might choose to purchase the rock for purely aesthetic reasons, or I might choose to disbelieve all known facts about the rock and hope for a different outcome ("even though it's never worked before, I am sure the rock will beat my gout!"), or I might make the purchase strictly on a whim for any or no reason whatsoever—this is my prerogative. But I cannot be scammed or defrauded, because I have access to all information regarding the transaction and the parties participating.

In general, then, I would posit that a loss of privacy will reduce crime not only because transparency acts as a deterrent but also because the underpinnings of many crimes rely on privacy.

De-Corrupting. Dis-Corrupting? Anti-Corruption? Something Like That

Similar to crimes of fraud, crimes that require potential revelation (blackmail/coercion), and crimes that are themselves a response to unwanted revelations (the Rajneeshee/Aum Shinrikyo/Jonestown murders), another major avenue of crime will be dispelled by loss of privacy: corruption.

Corruption can come in many forms, but perhaps the most straightforward and simple is government corruption: a person is granted a supernormal power (say, influencing the outcome of a court case or issuing a driver's license or awarding a contract) and receives some payment (which could be money or some nonmonetary reward) to use this power in a manner that serves a particular party.

For this to transpire, everyone involved requires secrecy; if the corruption is revealed, the people who are affected (that is, every member of the public, because the public granted the power to the government functionary) will react in a manner unfavorable to the corrupt participants.

There was a time when corruption had to be "rooted out," often, ironically, by using secrecy/deception to identify the corrupt parties. This was often the province of law enforcement agents or intrepid journalists or individual members of the public who had been aggrieved.[17]

---

[17] This included the two-year operation in which FBI employees dressed up as Arab sheikhs and, acting under instruction from a convicted felon who was given probation instead of jailtime for his part in the investigation, videotaped themselves bribing a number of American politicians; six Congressmembers and one Senator were eventually convicted, among many others. I know, a lot of this chapter seems fictional, but isn't.

Today, however, corruption is being revealed simply because the public has mobile recording devices and a way to share information quickly and widely.

In China, Internet users have been sharing images of public officials to determine if those officials may be corrupt . . . by examining the wristwatches they are wearing. Provincial work safety bureau head Yang Dacai, Railway Minister Liu Zhijun, and party secretary Bo Xilai were stripped of their positions, arrested, and prosecuted for corruption when, among other indicators, online activists identified their watches (and other personal luxury goods) as being too expensive to afford on their government salaries.[18] [19] [20]

> **NOTE**   I think there's also a significant likelihood that the online Chinese revelations are, in fact, also examples of how secrecy/privacy allows political machinations that go beyond public review of elected/ appointed officials. I'm going to guess that it's quite probably that the "online activists" who called out the corrupt officials for their wrist- watches were themselves agents of opposing political officials, acting to bring down these targets in a manner easy to explain and justify to the public.

A full loss of privacy would mean a corresponding total loss of the ability for the abuse of power that is corruption. Additional public over- sight is great and headed in the right direction, but an even better step would be to demand that our public servants open themselves up to *more* monitoring; I'd like to see every government employee wear a bodycam during working hours, in the same manner as police. I'd like constant access to every government computer, in real time—I own that computer (as do you, and all of us), and I paid for the work done on it and the data generated and stored there. I would certainly vote for the candidate who first offers to subject themselves to live monitoring, regardless of their politics.

---

[18] www.reuters.com/article/us-china-corruption/chinas-grinning-and-cor- rupt-watch-brother-gets-time-idUSBRE9840AC20130905

[19] moneyweek.com/merryns-blog/chinas-uneasy-realtionship-with-luxury-60114

[20] en.mercopress.com/2012/11/22/chinese-government-bankers-and-financers- warned-on-extravagant-and-lavish-expenditures

An End to Sabotage?

As with other crimes, total transparency means that the practice of sabotage would no longer be viable; everyone would be able to attribute every action to the specific persons/groups that took part. This would not only eliminate physical sabotage (property damage), but other forms of sabotage, such as affecting the integrity of data. Criminal activity in that realm includes actions such as election tampering, the spreading of false narratives, and unsubstantiated accusations (character attacks).

When we know the true source of all data, we are then able to interpret and understand the motivations and biases of those presenting the data. Did I really hear about that new movie from a friend, or from a marketing 'bot posing as my friend? Was that candidate really involved in a crime, or is the opposing candidate spreading that message in order to get my vote? Is there really an increase in death related to cholesterol, or are vegetable farmers trying to get me to buy more celery?

There was a significant amount of noise made about the 2016 elections in the United States. Much of it concerned the possibility that foreign governments, or agents of foreign governments, were spreading unfounded allegations about one candidate/party, because those foreign entities wanted the other candidate elected (for what reason, I was never quite sure; I don't think that was ever made clear by the accusers). There were calls to censor and regulate free expression to bring more honesty to elections.

First things first, anyone who thinks elections involve honesty, or ever have, has never heard a campaign promise.

Next, and perhaps most important, discouraging the flow of information about candidates is absurdly dangerous, especially when that power is granted to the existing government. If the government gets to choose which information we read, see, and hear about any candidates, obviously only laudatory information will be spread about incumbents and detrimental information about the opposition—power keeps power.

Moreover, I really don't care if the information I receive comes from foreign sources or local ones; if someone has something valuable to tell me about the candidate asking me for political power, I want to see that information. My fellow citizens are not supernaturally imbued with the only means to collect and parse useful data, so I'm willing to accept data from elsewhere. For instance, I know that a specific source trying to influence the elections is controlled by a foreign government that my country has fought at least two wars with, but every now and then the BBC offers some data of interest, so I don't think we need to prohibit them from taking part in the conversation.

There were also discussions about whether unattributed/misattributed/anonymous data elements were introduced into the public realm during the election and whether that should be "allowed." Again, giving censorship ability to the government will not in any way enhance free elections. And the ability to spread data anonymously is crucial when there is a power imbalance (between, say, corporation and employee, government and citizen, army and soldier, etc.); stifling anonymous sources eliminates the potential benefit we might derive from whistleblowers and informants. Of course, in a totally transparent world, this will not be an issue; everyone will know when an evil hypocrite like Macron tries to change reality by injecting selectively edited information into the public forum under a false name.[21]

In general, exposing the source of all data will not only address the issues brought up after the 2016 elections, it will remove the information-related disparities of power between all facets of society, legitimately.

Power Imbalance

Historically, central authorities have been the official recordkeepers of societies. Sometimes this was a religious entity, sometimes a dictatorship, sometimes an elected government. The authority would record births, deaths, property allocation, marriages, transactions, and the like.

These authorities gleaned power from this position: when what you write down is taken as legitimate fact, you can, to large extent, craft reality. Documentation is substantiation, and substantiation lends belief and credence; when you are in charge of the documentation (gathering, storing, tracking it), you can alter belief in what has occurred, and what hasn't, gravely affecting specific individuals and the society as a whole.

Oh, the parent of that child is not the peasant we thought it was, but is, in fact, part of the royal line? We can build an entire revolution around that child's claim to the throne. Oh, that property is actually owned by this family instead of that one? I guess the nonowners can

---

[21] See Chapter 6. Read it a few times. Macron's level of despicable behavior is worth multiple repetitions.

be evicted and disenfranchised. Oh, that person died of misadventure instead of suicide? Then they can be buried in this cemetery, and their family need not feel shame.

That creates a massive power imbalance between the populace and the central authority; the potential for corruption is staggering, and the hope of individual freedom and rights is negligible. A person cannot reasonably expect to stand as an equal against a government or religious organization or tribal elder when the former's reality is shaped by the latter's paperwork.

A lot of that power came from secrecy/privacy; the central authority had something the populace did not. The most basic hurdle was literacy; when an individual can't even create a record, much less review one for content and accuracy, the individual has no means of competing with the authority.

In a totally transparent society, where all data is shared with all members, that imbalance evaporates; if we can all see changes to the record, we can challenge them, disprove them, and refute them. Every individual's claim on reality is as strong as any other's; whether you work for the city court or as a plumber or as a software engineer, your words/data are equivalent in meaning and substance as anyone else's.

It seems wildly crazed, right? Allow complete data access to all citizens?

Some jurisdictions are moving in that direction already. DataSF is the city of San Francisco's program for crowdsourcing datasets. Since 2014, San Francisco has uploaded and created public access for a vast number of city databases and provided tools for analysis and manipulation of that data.[22]

In the intervening six years, San Francisco has not collapsed because city data has been made public. Of course, in our current quasi-private world, the city has not released *all* data, and a significant amount is still kept with the central authority. But the city (including the government, its citizens, and visitors) may continue to derive benefit through not only data transparency, but the ability to harness that data in novel ways that

---

[22] From the project's website: "DataSF's mission is to empower use of data. We seek to transform the way the City works through the use of data. We believe use of data and evidence can improve our operations and the services we provide. This ultimately leads to increased quality of life and work for San Francisco residents, employers, employees and visitors." datasf.org/opendata

would have been unpredictable by central planners. The project includes software/application development tools anyone can use to create their own app using the public data.[23]

This type of crowdsourcing leverages power, not the power of secrecy, but the power of human inquisitiveness and inventiveness, the urge to create and the urge to profit from your creation. A thousand private app developers can attempt new ways of utilizing data, over the same time frame that one city software project might make it through its first committee review *and at no cost to the taxpayers*—the cost of private development is limited strictly to those who want to invest their time and money in that particular effort. Anyone can benefit, everyone might benefit, and nobody is forced to finance the effort, whether it fails or succeeds.

The more data becomes exposed through loss of privacy, the more possible utility we might harvest from that data, through this kind of enterprise.

An End to Laws?

The United States has a lot of laws.[24] There are so many, in fact, that author and civil rights attorney Henry Silverglate has estimated that the average American commits three federal felonies every day, inadvertently.[25] Obviously, these laws are not all enforced evenly; some are never enforced at all. Why do we have them, then? More importantly, when all actions by all people are known to all others, how will the sheer number of newly detected crimes be prosecuted?

I'd be willing to bet any amount of money they won't. We simply do not have enough law enforcement/judicial/prison resources to prosecute and punish every crime currently on the books. In fact, that's kind of the situation, already. Choice of enforcement is left to the enforcers, and the prosecutors are allowed to determine which people to investigate,

---

[23] datasf.org/opendata/developers

[24] Seriously, we've got a federal law that prohibits any unauthorized person from using the likeness of Woodsy Owl. Title 16, Chapter 3, Subchapter 1, §580p-4. I am tempted to put a picture of Woodsy in this book, right here, in order to get arrested on federal charges as a publicity stunt. But I am a coward, so I won't. Chilling effect, demonstrated. Honestly, do younger readers even *know* what Woodsy Owl is???

[25] www.amazon.com/Three-Felonies-Day-Target-Innocent/dp/1594035229; I cannot recommend this book highly enough.

which crimes to charge and take to trial, and which sentences to recommend to the court.

This is obviously a flawed approach, open to vast effect by human frailty; prosecutorial decisions might be based on prosecutors' ego, grudges, predilections, and/or indifference. The prosecutor is put in the awkward position of trying to determine which crimes are the most "important," which are the most unpopular among the constituency, which are the most likely to be "successful" (where success is measured by conviction, not an amount of objective "justice"), and which are able to be accomplished with the resources at hand.

How, then, will the prosecutor choose to act when all crimes are recognizable and all evidence eminently available?

My guess—my hope—is that we will finally start paring down the vast number and scope of laws to something more rational and manageable. This is always difficult; politicians are often measured by the voting public based on the laws that the politicians create and lambasted for the laws the politicians remove. But, as mentioned in an earlier chapter, when Americans start to realize that all the crimes they might currently commit (online gambling, traffic violations, etc.) can and *will* be recorded for prosecution, Americans might begin to advocate for a change to the current overabundance of laws (and advocate for themselves, honestly, instead of pretending that they agree with most of these laws).

Fewer laws—fewer trials, fewer opportunities for mistakes, fewer people incarcerated, fewer pointless enforcement efforts. Perhaps it will lead to a time where authorities will only concentrate effort on activity that is meaningful or dangerous.

Perhaps.

Lower Costs

I don't think it's possible to measure the amount of money spent on securing data; there are simply too many different industries, organizations, and individuals making too many different kinds of expenditures that somehow play an INFOSEC role to properly account for them all. For instance, is the salary of a guard stationed in the lobby of a corporate headquarters building considered a privacy expenditure?

Suffice it to say, we spend a lot of money on privacy. We spend a lot of money trying to maintain privacy, trying to pierce privacy (through espionage activity), and both complying with and enforcing privacy rules and regulations. We spend money on privacy as individuals, as companies, and as taxpayers.

Worse: we spend our *time* supporting privacy/secrecy. There is a cost of convenience whenever we have to present multiple security factors (a password, a PIN, a thumbprint, a onetime code, etc.) to access data or take part in a transaction. Every single transaction might have a somewhat negligible cost of time (maybe five seconds, or ten), but these add up quickly and represent a substantial investment; if I log in to my bank online ten times a month and spend ten seconds verifying my identity each time, that's 20 minutes per year . . . and that's just for one vendor (my bank). I might conduct transactions with 300 vendors per year (hotels, airlines, retail companies, etc.), which might total 100 hours of my time, or two-and-a-half normal workweeks.

That's effort I'm expending that I get no remuneration for; it's work I'm doing for no reward. And I'm performing that work because my vendor has outsourced the work of securing my information—outsourced the work *to me*; I'm working to protect my own data, on behalf of someone I'm paying for something.

With the loss of privacy/secrecy, we can discount all those additional, extraneous costs: the cost of my time to secure my transaction, the cost of security controls for "sensitive" data that is no longer protected, the massive costs of military and espionage and security apparatuses that nation-states use to protect their own secrets and try to elicit secrets from other nation-states. Will there be costs (and risks) associated with transitioning from the current model to a non-private model? Again: yes, for sure. But I am willing to bet that the benefit in reduced costs will greatly exceed the potential harm, using any numerical metric.

An End to Hypocrisy

There's an even better benefit total transparency offers than saving money: thorough knowledge of everyone's actions compared to their words.

Loathing hypocrisy is an odd quirk of humanity. We can usually tolerate someone who disagrees with us, even if their opinion is directly counter to our own, and they are vehement (and even irrational) in their stance. However, someone who publicly states an opinion but acts directly counter to that statement, brings on themselves ridicule, derision, and a distaste bordering on abhorrence. This is especially true of lawmakers/politicians, who want to impose a set of rules on the populace but won't deign to follow those same rules themselves.

Total exposure will make this impossible; if everyone can observe everyone else's actions, we will know if the actions of a given person match their stated opinions. Someone who tries to impose an artificial limit on behavior, but engages in that behavior themself, will rightly be exposed and their propositions dismissed.

If you have insufficient self-control to maintain your own behavior in a manner that does not harm anyone, to the point you need to have the threat of force to keep you from engaging in certain activities, go hire someone to use force against you, or check yourself into a facility where your actions will be under constant control; do not impose your weaknesses upon us.

Which brings us to . . .

An End to Bad Policy

Right now, with secrecy and privacy, we can create flawed foundations on which to structure a society that does not serve the needs of individuals, nor the group as a whole. A significant portion of our cultural fabric is based on precepts couched as morality or misplaced sanctity. This is largely the result of vestigial shame left over from anachronistic religious imperatives or dogmatic mantras repeated regarding human behavior.

Believing in fantasies is bad enough; if someone wants to ignore reality, that's their right, as long as the only harm that might result is to themselves. (If you want, for instance, to disbelieve gravity and therefore choose to walk out a third-floor window instead of taking the stairs to the entrance on the ground, that's your prerogative . . . but try not to land on anyone passing by below.) But trying to impose those fantasies on others, for whatever reason, by force or coercion or persuasion, can result in terrible policies and practices.

There are many types of this sort of fantasy, but, as with shame, they mostly involve bodily functions of one type or other . . . typically ingestion and sex. There are some, however, that deal strictly with entertainment. Of course, as is usual for the tableau that is humanity, we also have some social fabrications that involve a combination of bodily functions and entertainment.

Some of these societal policies are questionable, and many are just downright fallacious. To name just a few, using only those that have been championed in my own lifetime:

- Masturbation is harmful.
- Music can be harmful.
- Art can be harmful.
- Literature can be harmful.
- Comedy can be harmful.
- Video games cause violence.
- Texting is harmful.
- Campaign promises are meant.
- Having a child is fun.
- Recycling is the best allocation of resources.
- Marijuana is dangerous.
- Drugs destroy society.
- Gambling destroys society.
- Altruism/suborning oneself to a collective is good for both the collective and the individual.
- Living life in pursuit of pleasure is bad for both the collective and the individual.

When I started writing this list, I meant to include just a few examples that I could expound on to demonstrate how transparency could diminish the ill effects of poor policy choices. I quickly found that the list would continue for pages if I didn't just arbitrarily stop typing. Now that I've created a list that probably offends absolutely everyone by challenging at least one cherished belief that you and I share, I'm going to try to continue the discussion of the topic.

Most of us will recognize at least one of the things on the list is fatuous. Some of them are relics of some bygone, primitive era that had a very different moral code (perhaps, a time when printing the word *fuck* in a book meant for public sale could get you thrown in prison, but owning a human being as property was allowed). Most of us will also recognize that more than one thing on that list is simply untrue . . . although we are reluctant to admit it to others, or discuss it, or even consider it in our own minds with any depth or objectivity.

While it's quite risky to make assertions of totality ("all" or "nothing" pronouncements), I'm going to guess that all of us realize the difficulty that will occur as these beloved norms/beliefs are proven wrong. While we're evolving our culture from pre-transparency to post-private, we're going to have to deal with the reality that many widely shared illusions cannot withstand the degree of scrutiny that such transparency provides.

To demonstrate this, I'm going to choose something from the list for which there is adequate and reasonable substantiation . . . and which most of us already suspect, instinctually: "video games cause violence." Probably because that is very near and dear to my own heart (the games, I mean, not the violence).[26]

Almost every entertainment medium has been accused of making juveniles do bad things: comic books,[27] music,[28] role-playing games,[29] television[30] . . . I suspect that there was probably a group of cave-parents who decried this new-fangled trend of "painting" violent images, as it was causing the kids to act up and misbehave. Video games seem to be a perennial favorite target for this kind of attention, though; where jazz, heavy metal, rap music, Wonder Woman, D&D, and cartoons seem to have been largely accepted by all but the fussiest of parents and societal crusaders, the hunt to prove that video games are the source of juvenile delinquency has ranged over multiple decades and doesn't seem to be waning anytime soon.

The American Psychological Association (APA), for instance, has been pecking at this notion for more than 40 years and seems to, at this point, take the proposition as granted[31] [32] (oddly, though, while they firmly state their belief that kids are made into violent monsters by video games, the shrinks only seem to suggest that the proper course of action is for the government and charities to give more money to APA members so they can do more "research"). Their counterparts across the Atlantic at the Royal Society, however, refute these findings.[33] More

[26] Full disclosure: I live to play video games and have worked as a play tester for a game company.

[27] slate.com/culture/2008/04/the-campaign-against-comic-books.html

[28] www.joesapt.net/superlink/shrg99-529/index.html

[29] www.popularmechanics.com/culture/gaming/a20453/moral-panic-dungeons-dragons; Also, check out Tom Hanks in *Mazes and Monsters* if you're bored or if you can find a way to watch it.

[30] apnews.com/80e11883effaad46e7b34b72803950a8

[31] www.apa.org/news/press/releases/2015/08/violent-video-games.pdf

[32] www.apa.org/pi/families/review-video-games.pdf

[33] Przybylski AK, Weinstein N. 2019 Violent video game engagement is not associated with adolescents' aggressive behaviour: evidence from a registered report. R. Soc. open sci. 6:171474.

importantly, the two most credible metrics for violent crime statistics in the United States (the FBI's annual report and the Bureau of Justice Statistics) have tracked a considerable drop in violent crime between 1990 and 2018.[34] If video game usage has markedly grown to the point of ubiquity during this same period and the premise is true ("video games cause violence"), we'd expect to see massive increases in violent crime, instead of the opposite.

> **NOTE**   There does seem to be some considerable link between playing video games (and perhaps more so violent video games) and "aggression," where the research has measured aggression using increased blood pressure, skin conductivity, and respiration. I find it interesting (and not a little ironic) that these same metrics might also describe the effects of "exercise." More interesting, I would be quite keen to learn the results of similar studies performed on other activities requiring engagement of the participant, and even more so if those activities were competitive (as many video games are, whether the competition is with computer-controlled 'bots, or other players). Anecdotally, I have seen grown men (in some cases, *elderly* men) do things with and to golf clubs that could not be described as anything other than "aggressive" . . . and certainly would be suited to the descriptor "violent."

Of course, "violence" is not the same as "violent crime"; it is possible to be violent without participating in a crime—I can punch a wall instead of a person, for instance. It's hard to measure victimless violence, though, and when someone claims the linkage "video games cause violence," it's usually the shrill cry of a blame-placer (a politician or an activist or just someone who hates fun on the principle that it's enjoyable) trying to convince us that games are ruinous to society. Moreover, the drive to create this link has led to all sorts of illogical reasoning, usually conflating correlation with causation and specious reasoning. Filmmaker Michael Moore spotlights one such hysterical claim in the movie *Bowling for Columbine*: while the school shooters Dylan Klebold and Eric Harris did, in fact, play video games (making

---

[34] www.pewresearch.org/fact-tank/2019/10/17/facts-about-crime-in-the-u-s; There are, however, at least two spikes marking increases of violent crime during this period, but they appear to be very temporary.

them not dissimilar from the majority of their cohort, including the children they shot), it would be just as sensible to blame their murder spree on the activity of bowling, which they participated in just hours before the rampage (that is to say, it would make no sense at all).

With full and open transparency, however, such illusory and super-stitious beliefs could not fester, and we would have to contend with the possibility that some people (including some children) are prone to violence . . . sometimes with no predicating sign or action and with no simple causative factor to blame.[35] We would know the totality of people who engage in one activity (video games) and the totality of those who engage in violent crimes (violent criminals), and we could also deter-mine the chronological proximity of the events (gaming and crimes), the rate of both an individual participated in, and so forth. In fact, we're fairly close to having this level of knowledge right now; most people, however, do not consider the data and instead prefer to subscribe to the shorthand of the myth.

However, one area where increased transparency has already had an effect on this particular illusion is regulation: government attempts to curtail free expression in the video game format have declined as more data demonstrates the lack of direct connection between games and crime. Previous efforts to control expression effected certain changes in how games are marketed and distributed: Congressional hearings in 1993 and 1994 culminated in a threat by Congress against gamemakers, that a new law called the Video Game Rating Act would be applied to that industry. Instead, the industry created the Entertainment Software Ratings Board (ESRB) to head off government censorship (in much the same way as the comic book industry did with the Comic Ratings Board decades prior). In 2003, the specter of government control of expression reared again, as a couple of US Senators proposed the Family Entertain-ment Protection Act (FEPA), which would grant the federal government the ability to control expression in game formats.[36] (FEPA got as far as the appropriate committee, but expired there with no further action.) In 2006, two Senators again proposed a federal law, but this one was only

---

[35] As with the case of Stephen Paddock, a 64-year-old former postal carrier, IRS agent, and accountant with no criminal record or history of violence. Paddock massacred more than 50 people in Las Vegas during the most deadly single shooting spree in the United States.

[36] www.cnet.com/news/senators-target-graphic-video-games

meant to fund studies by Centers for Disease Control and Prevention (CDC) into the "psychological effects" of games on kids.[37]

In 2011, the Supreme Court struck down a California law that would have prevented or regulated the sale or distribution of games to minors; in this decision, the Court unequivocally defined games as "protected speech," requiring Constitutional protection, and likened games to "books, plays, and movies."[38] The Court specifically noted the lack of data supporting the myth: "Any demonstrated effects are both small and indistinguishable from effects produced by other media." In 2018, a private meeting between game makers, industry representatives, and elected officials at the White House resulted in nothing very much at all: no new laws proposed or threatened, and no sweeping generalizations about the evils of gaming.[39]

It would seem, then, as accurate data becomes ubiquitous, the potential for creating policy based on *bad* data (myths and illusions) decreases.

Policies based on premises that are inherently wrong lead to unintended consequences, create burdensome and unnecessary costs, and stifle human activity and expression; without privacy/secrecy, it will be much easier to acquire hard data that accurately reflects human behavior. The reduction of privacy will allow acquisition of survey/ research data that truly depicts how people behave, instead of relying on the often-faulty technique of, first, finding potential candidates to take part in a voluntary study and then eliciting truthful and complete answers (a process made all the more difficult when the research topics involve any activity that might be considered shameful, embarrassing, revealing, or otherwise troublesome). As mentioned in Chapter 5, privacy/secrecy tends to skew data and can result in negative effects for what should be objective goals: policy, science, and medicine.

Speaking of Accurate Portrayals of Humanity . . .

Privacy also allows another type of harmful fiction: people with derogatory biases (e.g., racism, sexism) can operate among a society where

---

[37] www.gamespot.com/articles/views-clash-at-senate-game-hearing/1100-6146902

[38] www.supremecourt.gov/opinions/10pdf/08-1448.pdf

[39] www.gamespot.com/articles/president-trumps-video-games-meeting-included-a-vi/1100-6457255

those views are generally disgraced. Without privacy/secrecy, everyone would be able to readily identify those people who act on those distasteful beliefs, and we would all be better able to make choices based on our own beliefs. For instance, if I could choose where to purchase a particular good/service and the potential vendors included someone who supported racist causes, I might opt to buy from the nonracist vendor.

This already occurs, to some extent, at a microcosmic level, when a particular individual is revealed to hold some view/take some action that is perceived as untoward by the community at large. For instance, in 2014, Mozilla's CEO stepped down amid controversy, when attention was drawn to his choice of campaign contributions, which included donations to political groups that worked against efforts to create legal recognition of gay marriages. This public attention culminated in a dating website (OKCupid, one of the most popular such sites at the time) denying its users access if they were using Mozilla's browser, Firefox.[40]

There's a larger discussion to be had about this topic, one that could fill more than one entire book itself: should a person's private forms of expression have an influence on how they are perceived professionally, can a person hold irrationally biased beliefs and still act in an unbiased manner, is having an irrational bias necessarily morally loaded ("bad") in and of itself? And books have already been written about the more general case: can we separate, and enjoy, the fruits of someone's work, even if they are truly reprehensible in their personal life?[41]

But there's one particular element of total transparency and knowledge of the personal actions of everyone else that can only be resolved as we evolve through the transition from a quasi-private world: if someone has an irrational bias but acts with sufficient diligence to avoid displaying it, is that a benefit (to that person, and to humanity)?

No matter what level of exposure we end up with, we have no definitive means of reading someone's mind, and it's unlikely that such technology will be developed any time soon. So someone could, theoretically, hold some innate bias, be aware that their own bias is shameful, and therefore exert self-discipline such that the bias is never displayed in any way that could be observed.

Is that beneficial, or desired? In monitoring each other's actions, thereby affecting each person's behavior, are we achieving a world we

---

[40] blog.mozilla.org/blog/2014/04/05/faq-on-ceo-resignation
[41] See: Bill Cosby, Roman Polanski, etc.

want or just the preferred façade? In Orwell's *1984*, for instance, it's the latter outcome that is sought by the Party: by changing how everyone behaves, the government intends to change how everyone *thinks*, to the point where even the thought of rebelling against the collective is impossible. By conditioning the behavior of the populace, to the point where the citizens cannot even formulate the thoughts necessary to throw off their shackles, the oppressive regime maintains its own power.

Or . . . is it possible we will come to a different realization—that exerting the necessary discipline to hide our own biases simply requires too much effort, that we can't reasonably disguise our true selves and cease trying . . . thereby exposing ourselves, completely, to any and all who may want to observe, even when that exposure includes distasteful activity/ beliefs? Will we use this knowledge of each other to take turns belittling someone who does not conform to the perfect model of the current behavior set? Or might we recognize that everyone, to some degree or other, at some time or other, engages in an unpleasant behavior, but that this does not describe the totality of a person's character and humanity? Might we become more forgiving of the shortcomings of others when our own are fully displayed?[42]

I have no idea. I get the feeling the transition will be dreadful and awkward, especially for everyone who is already an adult in the quasi-private world. But, again, it is probably best to start this conversation now, instead of waiting for the moment we've already had total transparency thrust upon us by technology and innovation.

Vestigial Shame

Soon, in a post-private world, the only "shame" left will be the context-shame of unpopular acts. This sounds redundant, because it may seem as if that is already what we have: society/culture creates rules/mores/ cues based on the sort of activities the group detests/lauds . . . that is, prohibitions for the detestable stuff, encouragement for the laudable stuff. It would make sense, then, that shame is used to enforce the prohibitions, and acclamation for the desirable outcomes.

But that's not what we have in reality, because of privacy and secrecy. Instead, shame is weaponized against behavior we *say* we don't like,

---

[42] I'm reminded of the lyric from the musical *Avenue Q*: "Everyone's a little bit racist, sometimes."

instead of behavior we actually do not like. For instance, as a culture/society/government, we *say* we cherish monogamy as an ideal, but, in fact, very few of us practice lifetime monogamy.

NOTE Statistics for tracking monogamy/infidelity are incredibly fuzzy and tough to pin down, for several reasons.

- Context-shame and self-shame both contribute to the very real possibility that research/surveys/studies are tainted by incorrect data if they rely on self-reporting (and there's really no other way to gather that data).
- What one person frames as "infidelity," another will consider otherwise; for instance, some respondents to studies consider "viewing pornography" as "infidelity," while others only count "sexual contact with another person."
- Data about American marriages/divorces, for instance, are readily available[43] (probably because they require legal action/government sanction) and suggest that lifetime monogamy is highly unlikely *without* counting extramarital affairs, because there are continually almost half as many divorces as marriages, so it's likely that at least 50 percent of Americans will never be monogamous for their whole lives, but this data might not reflect a somewhat higher number of monogamous individuals, simply because one person can get married and divorced multiple times.
- Consensual nonmonogamous relationships (that is, individuals who agree to polyamorous arrangements) might not be considered "infidelity" by the participants and the subset of the population who recognize such relationships, but are less likely to be counted or tabulated in research/studies . . . and are, by definition, not geared toward the monogamous "ideal."

It seems much more likely that the concept of lifelong monogamy was one of those shared policies we, as a culture, created and maintained, and that the target was not so much monogamy in and of itself, but was more likely, "don't get caught by your declared partner or anyone your declared partner knows, and we will continue as if nothing happened." And, indeed, there seem to be many beneficial purposes for this, to include continued

---

[43] www.cdc.gov/nchs/data/dvs/national-marriage-divorce-rates-00-18.pdf

resource provision for children (who might be the product of infidelity), maintenance of long-term partnered relationships (even with extramarital sexual activity), and generally an acceptance that dalliances might not rise to the harm of ending an otherwise-viable marriage/relationship.

The end of privacy will destroy this perception; it will become immediately apparent that lifelong monogamy might, in fact, be the vast exception to human behavior, and not the rule (or even a goal likely to ever be achieved, except by wild outliers).

As privacy declines and information becomes more ubiquitous, technology evolution has made such utilities as mail-order genetic testing ubiquitous and commonplace. Knowing your genealogy allows an individual to possibly anticipate likelihood of certain medical conditions, satisfy personal curiosity about origins, and locate relations. It will (and has been used to) also dispute oral family histories, countering them with definitive proof instead of convenient fabrications.

Some jurisdictions, realizing the general upheaval this could cause for traditional arrangements (such as marriages and other pro-monogamous relationships, and the allocation of resources for children), have already taken steps to outlaw the practice/technology.[44] As with all societies that have tried to continue restrictive practices and stave off growth of personal freedom, this effort is a forlorn hope, unless the governing power is willing to deploy overwhelming force against both its own populace, its neighbors, and any other entity in the world, to shield its populace from individual choices.[45]

Again, access to more (and, eventually, all) data will reveal the truth, whether or not we're ready to accept the facts or to respond in a responsible manner. It would be best to begin that dialogue now, or to prepare for the revelations, *before* it occurs and the results are thrust upon us.

Vestiges in Action

We already know the extent of the damage that complete knowledge of revealed truths can cause: in 2015, AshleyMadison.com, an online

---

[44] France has done so, through both legislation and court decisions, for more than a decade. Of course, it's *France*. www.statnews.com/2019/11/14/france-consumer-genetic-testing-ban

[45] North Korea, for instance, is willing to expend that kind of effort. France probably won't . . . and, in the long term, French citizens will avail themselves of these technologies, legitimately or otherwise.

service for finding extramarital sexual partners, was hacked, with the attacker(s) collecting massive amounts of user and operational data.

The hacker(s) were not, themselves, extorting anyone or any entity for money, originally. The attacker(s) used the name "The Impact Team" and sent a threat to the owners of AshleyMadison.com, demanding that the site (and another site owned by the same company, for the same general purpose) be taken down. In the demand The Impact Team made to the website owners, the attacker(s) stated extreme dissatisfaction that the service was unethical, for a number of reasons.[46]

- The company promised users total privacy, forever, but the hack demonstrated this promise was impossible to maintain.
- The company promised total deletion of a user's account upon request, but then charged a fee for the deletion *and* did not fully delete the user's account.
- The company was profiting from human misery and pain.

NOTE An even more bizarre detail: the attacker(s) apologized, by name, to the director of security for AshleyMadison.com, saying, "You did everything you could, but nothing you could have done could have stopped this."

The site's owners did not comply with the attacker(s)' demands by the time of the deadline; the attacker(s) then published this data publicly, revealing it to a global audience.

Within weeks, users of the service were receiving extortionist threats.[47] Six days after the data was exposed, a New Orleans pastor killed himself, admitting in a note to his family that he was ashamed of his participation in the online service.[48] Other deaths would later also be attributed to the revealed data (though direct linkage was not as obvious and clear-cut).

There's an abundance of weirdness happening in this example. The extortionists were operating under a reliance on an extra layer of

---

[46] blog.malwarebytes.com/cybercrime/2015/08/for-sign-off-times-up-ashley-madison-data-released

[47] krebsonsecurity.com/2015/08/extortionists-target-ashley-madison-users

[48] money.cnn.com/2015/09/08/technology/ashley-madison-suicide/index.html

privacy: the privacy of data abundance, mixed with human laziness. Meaning, the blackmailers threatened to reveal a user's participation to that user's family/employers, but that threat was viable only if the user's family/employers had *not already gone and looked at the public data.* Basically, the extortionists were selling something that couldn't be delivered: privacy. The victim's family/employers would have to sort through hundreds of thousands of names to find the victim listed, and the blackmailers were counting on most people not being willing to exert that effort, sans prior suspicion.

The leaked data also revealed some other pretty egregious behavior on the part of AshleyMadison.com.

- According to internal emails, company executives illegally hacked a competitor's IT environment, prior to negotiating a merger/acquisition of the competitor.[49]
- While the service purported to connect men and women for the purpose of arranging extramarital affairs, it seems that the company was, instead, actually just exploiting male customers; 95 percent of the users were male customers, and the majority of the remaining 5 percent "female" customers, were actually fake accounts propagated by the company itself. Some of these fakes went beyond just having a profile/photo and instead used automated scripts to generate, send, and reply to messages from male users.[50]
- The owners of AshleyMadison.com were also well aware of rampant security vulnerabilities in the company's IT and had been warned by the company's security director weeks before the hack.[51]
- The hacked IT infrastructure was also used to store a variety of other sensitive materials, many completely unrelated to the company's operations, such as a scan of the CEO's driver's license and an AshleyMadison-themed movie script.[52]

---

[49] krebsonsecurity.com/2015/08/leaked-ashleymadison-emails-suggest-execs-hacked-competitors
[50] Annalee Newitz's amazing analysis of the exposed data revealed a great deal of information about the "fembots," including how they were programmed to persuade male users into purchasing more "credits" from AshleyMadison.com, gizmodo.com/ashley-madison-code-shows-more-women-and-more-bots-1727613924
[51] ibid, 35
[52] ibid, 35

■ Because the company did not verify that a user's email address actually belonged to the person registering it, anyone could create an account for any email address they knew (or imagined). (So, for instance, you, the reader, could create an account for ben@benmalisow.com.) However, anyone wanting to *close* an account with their own email address would be charged a fee, regardless of whether they, themselves, had created the account.[53]

The promise of privacy, anonymity, and secrecy created a situation rife for exploitation, and once transparency was forced on the participants (unwillingly, by a third party uninvolved in the transaction!), damage ensued, for pretty much everyone involved.

It's going to happen. Transparency is escalating (whether consensually or otherwise), and secrecy/privacy/anonymity is plummeting. Again, it's not my preference for this to happen, but it's going to happen nonetheless. And we'd be better prepared to contain and deal with the resultant damages if we have the necessary discussions about these topics and deal with the reality of our culture, society, and species, rather than painfully grasping at the illusions we've artificially maintained until now.

---

[53] theintercept.com/2015/07/21/ashley-madison-breach-why-am-i-getting-their-emails

The Upshot

8

"Stop children— what's that sound? Everybody look what's goin' down."
– Buffalo Springfield, For What It's Worth

The rest of this book has examined why total transparency may offer some benefits to humanity and how loss of privacy might not be a complete tragedy. In this chapter, I discuss how the segue between the quasi-private world and one of total transparency might occur.

This is almost certainly a boneheaded effort. Just about everyone who has ever tried to accurately predict *anything*, from weather to financial markets to elections[1] to human behavior, has been an utter flop; this is more true for technology and the cultural/societal impact of technology than just about every other prediction.[2] Yes, there have been a few people who have gotten a few things right, among a mass of predictions they, as individuals, have made[3]—there are even fewer—who have made a bunch of predictions and had them be mostly accurate.

Almost nobody can accurately predict what will happen with innovation and technology and how disruptive and/or beneficial a particular company/idea/invention might be. IT is a fairly young industry (unless we want to include tactile/hard-copy information tech, such as the abacus, literacy, the printing press, telegraph, and other pre-computer developments as "IT") and has experienced vast transitions for major

---

[1] *Especially* elections; for some reason, even though election predictors are notoriously, wildly inaccurate, we keep funding and believing polls. We, as a species, are particularly stupid and unscientific in this regard.
[2] fee.org/articles/the-great-horse-manure-crisis-of-1894
[3] Including Michael Burry, Harlan Ellison, and Mark Twain

participants; today's giant might be tomorrow's amoeba.[4] It's hard to imagine the current major players going out of business or being reduced to niche providers, but it wouldn't be unprecedented: less than 100 years ago, the largest retailer in the world was Woolworth's.[5]

In this chapter, I'm going to attempt the foolhardy effort of describing what some of the shapes of a transparent world might look like. Please forgive me if I end up looking like a complete idiot five years from now.

Science Fiction

I'm going to piggyback on the works of other writers who have explored these themes to try to expound on some of their concepts of what might drive the transparency transition and what the world might be like on the other side.

Vernor Vinge is not only one of my all-time favorite science-fiction authors, he's also a former professor of mathematics and computer science.[6] His idea of the "singularity" is often referenced in both fiction and nonfiction works, although, I think, not always portrayed accurately. As I understand it, Vinge's concept is that a "singularity" event is something that significantly and fundamentally changes human existence in a manner wholly previously unpredictable; a singularity event would not only affect philosophy and academic thought, but day-to-day life, as well. This has often been interpreted to mean that Vinge predicts that a truly self-aware artificial intelligence will challenge humanity; my understanding is that this definition limits the possible sources/causes of a singularity event—"the singularity" might not only be caused by machines attaining thought and competing with humanity, but any far-reaching, deeply affecting discovery or development (to include, maybe, total transparency or perhaps

---

[4]I still have an AOL email account and recall using a Hayes external modem, a Commodore 64, Compuserve, Prodigy, and shopping at ComputerWorld. Please note: I specifically did not say "fondly recall" about particular entries on this list.
[5]It has since all but faded into obscurity; there is still a chain of shops in Australia, and the Footlocker athletic shoe stores were a product of the original Woolworth's parent company. www.woolworthsmuseum.co.uk/aboutwoolies.html
[6]lccn.loc.gov/n84078385

cold fusion or teleportation or meeting an intelligent alien species or something else altogether).[7]

But the pertinent concepts I draw from Vinge's work aren't related to the singularity; instead, it's his notions of how people will use technology to interact with each other and the world that I find relevant to the discussion of transparency. In several of Vinge's works, the characters use wearable technology ubiquitously, specifically ocular implants/IT-enabled contact lenses that project information and take direction immediately from the wearer's eyes. (That is, instead of touching a keyboard/mouse/touchpad/screen, the user looks directly into the lens they wear in their eye(s) and enters input based on eye movements/staring.)

Vinge is not unique in suggesting this mode of IT interaction, and I don't think he pioneered the concept, but he may be the writer who most popularized the notion through his work, and it's certainly Vinge who made the idea most vivid to me.

We already have (or have had) primitive versions of this technology, both in the hardware implementation and in the use case. Our term for describing information that is visually presented to the user concurrently with actual optical information is *augmented reality* (AR) (somewhat different from *virtual reality* (VR), where all of the data the user sees is synthesized, and none of it comes directly from anything the user is actually looking at). An example of AR would be: first you look at a building, then you point a device at that building, and then you look through your device at the building, where you see not only the image on the screen containing the building but also raw data and/or links to other data about the building—maybe the date the building was constructed, the manufacturer's code for the particular color of paint used on that building, the assessor's value ascribed to the property by the jurisdiction that taxes it, the postal address or latitude/longitude coordinates of the building, and so forth. You see the building, but you also see additional visual information through the interface.

In Vinge's world, users and AR services go a step further: the user might choose what kind of information is overlaid on the real world. For instance, someone who enjoys children's fairy tales might see

---

[7]Vinge's paper, "The Coming Technology Singularity," lists four possibilities, including networked machines "waking up" (ala Skynet from the Terminator series of films) and natural human brainpower enhanced by cybernetic implementations; however, I don't think Vinge intended those four possibilities to be the exclusive singularity-type events. edoras.sdsu.edu/~vinge/misc/singularity.html

buildings as made of gingerbread instead of construction materials, and people might be depicted as mythical creatures like elves and ogres instead of their actual features—the user selects what kind of world they want to see, and the device portrays the world according to that selection. And if multiple users want to share the same "world," the service shows them identical AR depictions of the same buildings, people, streets, sky, etc.

How can this lead to transparency? As the devices/interfaces are presenting information to the user, they are also necessarily capturing information *about* the user: where the user is, the user's identity (even if that identity is limited to a username, instead of a name on a birth certificate or driver's license), what the user is looking at, how long they look at it, what appeals to them, how they choose to interact, who they interact with, and so on. Without the service having this information, the service would be useless; without the user opting to share that information with the service, the user would derive no benefit.

So users will gladly part with their data to gain the benefit of a pervasive, ubiquitous service that captures everything they look at. It's a natural evolution from current social media interactions and just reduces the barriers between what the user intends to share at any given moment (a photo, a video, some text) and the user's entire perceived existence.

Why hasn't this happened yet? Largely, because current users are too old to appreciate (or properly utilize) a fully ubiquitous interface they're not already familiar with . . . and because they're immensely reluctant to part with personal privacy, both as users and as *observable participants in public* (more on the latter in the next section). Age is a considerable factor; most adults are currently jealous of their privacy and want to limit who can and cannot collect information about them; they feel (rightly) that someone who can collect details about personal lives has influence and some degree of power over the subject of the surveillance, and that information gathered in this way can be used to cause harm. Of course, many of these adults also post photos of their infants, meals, and home on social media, accept software terms of service without reading them, and announce to the world travel plans, including the dates when they will be away from their home.

Each generation is incrementally more comfortable with technology, both in use and in effect; I get the feeling that the current (or very next) generation will be hard-sold on sharing even *more* personal data with the world and will rely even less on privacy (or, more accurately, promises of privacy).

Public Perception

This is an area where there is a massive disparity between the United States and large parts of the rest of the world; America's Constitution recognizes the human right of free expression, which includes capturing, recording, and broadcasting any event/image that transpires in public view. So, as an American, in American jurisdictions, I can take photographs/videos/recordings of whatever I want as long as what I'm documenting occurs in public (with some limited exceptions, which I'll address shortly).

If I want to walk around with my smartphone and take photos of everything I see, I can do so—I can post all the material I record to the Internet, as well, for everyone to see. I can attach my smartphone to a drone and send the drone flying around public airspace to document everything, too.[8] I can wear a bodycam and capture all my activities and interactions . . . in some states (in certain American states, I must inform anyone whose voice I'm recording that I'm capturing audio, prior to doing so, so if I wear a shirt that says, "I'm recording all audio," while wearing the bodycam, I will probably have a good defense against prosecution). I can record police officers in the process of policing.

Here's where things get weird: I can even attach a telephoto lens to my image/video recording device, and as long as I'm standing on public property (like a street or sidewalk), I can capture footage of you, inside your home, if you leave your curtains open. That is considered "public view."

So, in 2013, when Google created a wearable recording device known as Google Glass, it was perfectly legal to use in the United States. But a lot of people hated the very idea of it.

Google Glass was basically a bodycam that also featured a heads-up display (HUD); a pair of spectacles that projected information on the lenses for the user to see and a camera attached that could record whatever the user was looking at. Captured data could be stored locally on the device or uploaded to web-based storage; theoretically, any recordings

---

[8]See Chapter 6, about the Streisand Effect.

could then be rebroadcast by the user however the user chose (including publicly, on the Internet).

People *hated* it. Well, nonusers hated it. Users, typically early adopters who had the financial wherewithal and a desire to be trendy, seemed to really enjoy the functionality (even though it was somewhat lacking in terms of operational capability; the technological implementation didn't quite match the promise of concept). Nonusers started referring to users as "Glassholes."

If you don't like the product, you don't have to buy it and use it. What's the problem?

Many Americans did not like the idea of being under constant observation by everyone else around them and having their every interaction/ action recorded. This is understandable; I've already listed a host of dystopian portrayals of a surveillance state in this book, some fictional, some historical. Americans in 2013 (and 2014, when Glass was made widely available to the public, and not just a limited test audience) were jaded to the point of outraged about the possibility of attaining a surveillance state *voluntarily*, much less having it imposed upon them by a government.

Google discontinued public sale of the product in 2015. Glass is still available in an enterprise edition, for use in the workplace. (American employers, again much different than other parts of the world, can record *anything* that occurs in the workplace, with very few exceptions.[9])

If there was so much antipathy toward ubiquitous documentation of everyday life just a few years ago, why would I possibly think tomorrow, or next year, will be any different?

A lot has happened in the past few years. AR implementations have found use cases that have proven to be insanely popular, especially with younger user communities. For instance, a Pokemon-themed AR game, known as Pokemon Go, allowed users to interact with the world around them as part of the game; to participate in the game (which includes visiting real-world landmarks and map locations), users were required to share their own location data with the game service (and, in variations of the game, share their device's photo-capture capability). (Pokemon is a Japanese cartoon popular with young people.) At the height of its popularity, soon after its release, there were more than 28 million daily users of the game.[10]

---

[9]Notably: what goes on in bathrooms/changing rooms or the break room may not be recorded.

[10]www.businessofapps.com/data/pokemon-go-statistics

What changed?

For one thing, the target demographic of the customer: Glass catered to tech-aware, trendy adults, and required an expenditure of $1,500 to even get started as a user; Pokemon appeals to young people, and installing Pokemon Go on a smart device is free (if you don't put a price on the value of your privacy).

For another, what the device captured: while Glass ostensibly recorded images, video, and audio at any time the user triggered it (potentially without the awareness of nearby people), Pokemon Go captured location data of the user and photos (with an implied notice to nearby people; the user would be pointing their device at whatever was being captured).

I think the first element is actually the more important aspect, in terms of allowing market penetration and ubiquity of use; young people are probably more apt to be flippant or dismissive of privacy concerns and more likely to want to share their data online. They've been raised with technology older generations might otherwise perceive as intrusive. AR and VR are going to be inculcated in the lives' of the next generation in ways older people never conceived of.[11]

Our fears, our paranoia in approaching transparency, might not be passed on to the next generation, who might be more comfortable with a less private, more open existence.

Other Visions

Vinge, of course, is not the only speculative fiction author to have tackled the idea of AR or wearable electronics or a world in which real-time data is openly shared with either a large audience or the public as a whole. I just happen to like the concepts presented in his works that are relevant to this discussion.

I am reminded of other writers' works, however, that directly address the idea of what would happen, and what could happen, if everyone, everywhere, were instantly allowed to view/hear everyone else. Two short stories/novellas stand out for me: Isaac Asimov's "The Dead Past" and Damon Knight's "I See You."

In both stories, a dedicated inventor creates a device anyone can use to view anyone else, anywhere. Asimov's story ends abruptly with the

---

[11]There's a great podcast that includes a discussion of this topic, among others: pod-cast.wh1t3rabbit.net/dtsr-episode-373-things-your-phone-knows-about-you

reveal that such a device would utterly destroy privacy and fundamentally change society as we know it, without exploring much what those changes might entail.

Knight, however, prods at a few of those possibilities. And this is where the concept of losing privacy *without an end to civilization or descent into dystopia* manifests more than other works that feature diminished privacy. Knight's story includes an anecdote of what happens when a man realizes his wife is cheating on him, and his brother-in-law (his wife's brother) also realizes that the husband has just learned this information:

> In a house in Cleveland, a man watches his brother-in-law in the next room, who is watching his wife getting out of a taxi. She goes into the lobby of an apartment building. The husband watches as she gets into the elevator, rides to the fourth floor. She rings the bell beside the door marked 410. The door opens; a dark-haired man takes her in his arms; they kiss.

> The brother-in-law meets him in the hall. "Don't do it, Charlie."

> "Get out of my way."

> "I'm not going to get out of your way, and I tell you, don't do it. Not now and not later."

> "Why the hell shouldn't I?"

> "Because if you do I'll kill you. If you want a divorce, OK, get a divorce. But don't lay a hand on her or I'll find you the farthest place you can go."

This scene is particularly interesting because it echoes a theme used in other science-fiction works that treat similar situations as more inimical to humanity. In Spielberg's *Minority Report*, for instance, law enforcement responds to potential crimes before they occur, arresting and prosecuting the offender for what they may do later. The horrific potential in Spielberg's story is that someone will be punished *prior* to their action; in Knight's story, there is no punishment, only prediction and warning.

Knight's story, then, is more optimistic and hopeful than other, similar fictional works. Why does most literature tend toward postulating a post-private world that is hostile to personal freedom and dangerous to the individual? Is that simply a trope that sells more stories and titillates the reader more than a work that features a utopian ideal of harmony and personal fulfilment? There's very possibly an element of that in many of the most popular works: people enjoy being scared, or reading about conflict, much more than reading/watching stories about how swell everyone gets along and is happy. In fact, without conflict, you might not actually have a story to tell.

But I think there's more to our instinctual fear of transparency and the manifestations of it that writers use to tell stories: at the base of these fears is the dread that transparency will be inequitable and will put us, as individuals, at a disadvantage. A nation-state, a municipality, a community, an *employer* that knows all about you (while you know little about its secretive machinations) can impose on you; it can punish you, relentlessly and ubiquitously, for every infraction you've engaged in (and many you're planning), if your every move and word is captured and shared . . . and you have little recourse, because those monoliths are impenetrable to you. You have little or no access to the function and whims of the people engaged in enforcement and are therefore left at their mercy.

Quite possibly the best-known work that features a world without privacy is Orwell's *1984*; it's the template for all surveillance-state, fascist dystopias. It is quite possibly a perfect work of literature: it transcends location and time and handles deep questions about humanity and society in a very simple manner that is easy to grasp and understand, on both an intellectual and emotional level.

It's also utterly terrifying, not the least because of the description of what life is like for a human being under constant surveillance.

Why do I think a post-private world might be more like Knight's world than Orwell's? Because in *1984* or *Minority Report* or any other fictional work that features a surveillance state, or even in the real world, in historic oppressive states that used intrusive surveillance and reduced privacy, the terror comes not from exposure, but from an entity that has exclusive ability to monitor individuals—that is, *the individual is subject to monitoring by others, but does not likewise have that ability to monitor them.*

I think it's this aspect, the disproportionality of observation, which causes the fear and creates (a very real and rational) terror that the individual will be powerless/helpless before the entity that has this capability, but is shrouded from the individual. If we were all (every individual) at data parity . . . if we could all see what everyone else (where "everyone" could be "each person" or "each agency" or "each company") is doing, no one entity would have advantage over any person; uniformity of knowledge creates an insulation for everyone. If I know just as much about the police chief and the lead prosecutor and the head of a data-mining company as they know about me, their ability to prosecute me diminishes (as does their motivation to do so). Attempts to exploit me dissipate even as they are conceived. Any vulnerability I have is shared by every other person—and we all have knowledge of each others'.

In both Orwell's and Spielberg's works (and other fictional descriptions of dystopias, such as *The Hunger Games*), the entity that surveils without being observed is the government, but modern fears of inequitable privacy aren't limited to state-sponsored surveillance; today, we worry just as much that tech giants, conglomerates, medical providers, app-makers, and telecommunications services have the same kind of disproportionate inspection of our information, while we have little insight into theirs. Right now, that's definitely true: companies that provide computing and communications services have more data collection, processing, and storage capability than any individual can reasonably, effectively, and financially deploy and utilize.

But that's changing rapidly—there's a point of diminishing returns when it comes to managing large volumes of data; bigger is only better for as long as the data can be managed in a way that offers value (again, one needle, a million haystacks, and clipping level). After that, it's just a collection of data. And technology is actually working in favor of the individual users: a single person's capabilities are quickly accelerating to be on par with those of the largest tech purveyors. Gordon Moore, one of the foundational members of the microchip manufacturing industry, predicted (in 1975) that the number of components in an integrated circuit would double every two years. Effectively, he was predicting that computer processing capabilities, for commercially available computers, would escalate rapidly and continue to grow. And, for a long time, Moore's law held, usually exceeding the pace of the prediction. This means significant levels of processing capacity have become ubiquitous for all users; more data can be accessed and manipulated by an individual today than entire nation-states could reasonably process just 70 years ago. Concurrent developments in marketing and distribution of expanded data storage and processing capabilities, as well as virtualization (providing abstracted access to hardware perceived through the user's software interface), have created "cloud" computing: an individual with a credit card can rent tens, hundreds, or thousands of machines to perform whatever computational tasks the user wants. Capacity may or may not continue to escalate; we may reach a time where the physical limits of the chipsets maxes out performance, or we may shift to new physical substrates like graphene (instead of silicon) that will offer advances beyond what even Moore's law promised. Likewise, advances in quantum computing may increase the speed of electronic calculation far beyond current capabilities,[12] in devices that are small and cheap enough such that every person could have their own . . . approaching parity of capability for every individual and organization. At some point, size doesn't matter; a billion quantum computers don't have an appreciable advantage over *a* quantum computer, in terms of what can actually be accomplished. The limits, at that point, are related to access to data: if you and I both have access to a quantum computer and you have access to more data than me, you have an advantage—if we have the same access, we are at parity. (Now, if I choose to use my quantum computer to watch cat videos and you use yours to plot trends in consumer habits, you'll probably make more money, but I'll chuckle more.)

The one thing that maintains disproportionality of access is regulation; we have seen in recent months/years that the larger providers are all making public statements very much in favor of additional increased regulation over how information is treated and handled. The simple reason for this is: as long as regulation makes compliance difficult, only the larger entities will manage to be compliant; smaller entities and individuals will be kept in line (and out of access) by the enforcers, because they won't be able to afford compliance. (See Chapter 6 for more reasons why continued and enhanced regulation isn't the solution to any privacy question.)

---

[12]In the past few years, several tech firms have announced that they have quantum machines and are fielding them for commercial use. As with most nascent technology, the field is moving in fits and starts, and the capability is far from ready for wide use right now. Players include IBM [newsroom.ibm.com/2019-01-08-IBM-Unveils-Worlds-First-Integrated-Quantum-Computing-System-for-Commercial-Use#assets_115:1612], Honeywell [spectrum.ieee.org/tech-talk/computing/hardware/honeywell-claims-it-has-most-powerful-quantum-computer], and Google [www.reuters.com/article/us-alphabet-quantum/google-unveils-quantum-computer-breakthrough-critics-say-wait-a-qubit-idUSKBN1X21QW], among others.

Without additional regulation protecting the powerful entities and with advances in technology, we're fast approaching a time when every individual will have the same data collection/processing/storage capacity as the major players. And that's when transparency sidesteps dystopia.

Molecular Level

So far, most of the surveillance I've discussed (and most of what we think of) involves video and auditory monitoring—cameras and microphones. But there are so many other ways to gather data, in a much more exhaustive and extensive manner, that we're only scratching the surface of total transparency at the moment. What else could we do if we had nigh-infinite means to collect, store, and process data?

Let me step further into the realm of science fiction . . . which is a term preferable to "prediction."

Right now, every molecule in the universe has a position; in a moment, they will all be in new positions— at the molecular level, nothing is static. As they move, they brush against other molecules, and the reactions of those molecules are distinct and measurable. At a micro level, your hand sweeping by the candle puts out the flame. At a macro level, the butterfly's wings beating can be linked to an eventual typhoon in China.[13]

If we were to capture the position of every molecule right now and then a moment from now, we'd have two points on a continuum; with two points, we can start to draw a line. With three points, or three billion points, we could map a world. With some really good math and enough data, we could track the most probable path backward from each molecule to see where it was in the moment *before* we took the first data snapshot . . . and the moment before that and the moment before that. The movement of molecules is just a study of probabilistic likelihoods: what is the most likely position those molecules were in, the moment before now? Before then? Before then?

---

[13]Some science fiction refers to this literally as the *butterfly effect*, and there is heavy use of it in the literature to demonstrate causation. I tend to think of it more as correlation: would the typhoon have occurred sans the butterfly flapping? Probably—the flapping was just one input, and the result would likely occur without it.

Boiling this down: the ability to see into the past is simply a matter of having enough processing capacity to do the math.[14]

We wouldn't be able to interact with the past; it wouldn't be a "time machine" per se. More like a time viewer. And it couldn't readily predict the future, because there are far too many random and pseudo-random occurrences that would change the positions of molecules in unpredictable ways. Even if we ditched the notion of human free will and assumed predestination, any form of life that include movement injects randomness into the equation, because of imperfection (we might predict a cat and a rodent will cross paths, and there's a likelihood the cat will pounce at the rodent, but how far the cat jumps, how quickly, how it lands . . . these are open to variables; also, it's a cat, so it may just decide to not jump).

But we could see what everyone has done and hear everything they've said (sound is just molecules bumping into each other). In Technicolor, 3D, Dolby, and Sensorama. We could statistically reenact the entirety of history, with total knowledge.

It's just a matter of calculating power and math. It won't happen any-time soon. I am comforted somewhat by the idea I'll be dead before it happens. Most likely, anyway.

There are a host of other nonvisual, nonaudio technologies that might be used (or are being used) for surveillance purposes. Electromagnetic radiation may be feasible: microwave, extremely high frequency, and extremely low frequency emissions might be used to flood an area and measure obstructions/delays of the signal (to include the location of people). Outside the visual spectrum, we already use infrared (IR) and ultraviolet (UV) sensors to view people. Pressure sensors belowground can measure human footsteps (and determine weight of the person); laser motion sensors can track and map shapes. Acoustic waves (beyond audible sound) can map areas and content of those areas.

In short, surveillance sensors, and gathering data, can be done in a myriad of ways that go far, far beyond whatever can be seen, heard, or logged through communications traffic. These are improving in sync with all our other technology. As calculation and data storage capabilities increase in pace with sensor tech, privacy is dissipating, and transparency approaches.

---

[14]We'd have to calculate all the possible previous positions of the molecules and then calculate the one position (or set of positions) that was the most probable to have occurred. So, both physics and statistics.

Busting My Hump

A post-private world is particularly dangerous to me; I live off the idea that some data is private. I sell information in the form of books; people pay for access to the information. If all data, everywhere, and all human activity becomes observable to everyone else, it's possible I will lose sources of revenue; if everyone can access my books without paying me, I will have done a lot of work for no recompense.

Won't this be extremely troublesome to everyone who creates intellectual property—that is, creative expressions of data or inventions or novel techniques, or formulae? If anyone can see all data, won't that devalue all data?

Not necessarily. I'm not completely worried that the data I create will become worthless in a post-private world. For a few reasons.

Style Over Substance

For one thing, the way data is packaged is just as important (if not more so) as its content. I offer an example of a previous paragraph:

> A POST-PRIVATE WORLD IS PARTICULARLY DAN-
> GEROUS TO ME; I LIVE OFF THE IDEA THAT SOME
> DATA IS PRIVATE. I SELL INFORMATION IN THE
> FORM OF BOOKS; PEOPLE PAY FOR ACCESS TO THE
> INFORMATION. IF ALL DATA, EVERYWHERE, AND
> ALL HUMAN ACTIVITY, BECOMES OBSERVABLE TO
> EVERYONE ELSE, IT'S POSSIBLE I WILL LOSE SOURCES
> OF REVENUE; IF EVERYONE CAN ACCESS MY BOOKS
> WITHOUT PAYING ME, I WILL HAVE DONE A LOT OF
> WORK FOR NO RECOMPENSE.

Even though it's the same data, it's hard to read: it's ugly, it's misshapen, and it's not easy to get through. The way it's presented matters; a book has value not only because of what it contains, but how it is presented. (Don't ever tell this to my publishers/editors; I refuse to admit that they are anything other than parasites, as a proper negotiating stance.) The same can be said of the way other media is packaged, as well; music/television/movies are more enjoyable, and less jarring, when they do not contain advertising interruptions, which is why we are willing to pay a premium for a non-intrusive experience.

So I think there will still be value to be had in creating data, even in expressive works. People are willing to pay premium prices to sit with a crowd of other people in uncomfortable seats to see a Broadway show live, instead of via a screen in the comfort of their own home. Ditto concerts, comic performances, plays, and so forth. Some people are content to watch others play games (and the players are often paid to advertise products or services); others are willing to pay a premium to participate in the game. Some people are willing to pay to watch a movie on a big screen that would not fit into their home.

There's a flipside to this, of course. Earlier in the chapter, I mentioned that there are some exceptions to how data (images/video/audio) may be captured in public and rebroadcast under the legal framework of the United States. Some of those limitations feature extremely distasteful aspects of human behavior, and transparency will facilitate those. Openness is not a magical cure-all for all social ills.

For instance, the perception of the viewer of the data might lead to criminal infractions for otherwise legitimate data, depending on the biases and sensibilities of the person viewing the material. Parents have been arrested, and children taken into state custody, for photos that have including bathing their infant children and breastfeeding.[15]

So, total transparency may create opportunities for people to gather data that may be used in a manner we find disconcerting; it may be difficult to detect and impossible to control. You and I might look at a painting of Saint Sebastian made in the 1500s; one of us sees a piece of religious iconography and art history, while the other sees a depiction of eroticism tinged with pedophilia, necrophilia, and torture porn. Transparency gives the eyes of the beholder a wide latitude to derive their own value from any data, whether or not other beholders appreciate or approve of that value.

The Added Value of the Long Reach

Another reason I'm not overly dreading the end of data privacy is because total access will also mean wider audiences, and more possibilities for realizing value.

The wider audiences will be truly global; translation service continues to grow apace other technologies, and the limitations of a printed book (a set text, in a certain language, with a defined format) won't similarly

---

[15]www.dallasobserver.com/news/1-hour-arrest-6419852

impinge on the readership of digital data—people from anywhere, using any language, can access electronic books in a way (and at a speed) hard copy could never achieve. Content creators don't have to wait until a book is printed, the reels of a film are copied, or music is recorded onto a physical medium; distribution via online platforms is instant and total.

While the content of a book might not garner the purchase price it once did, the value of the book won't be completely degraded for the author; an author might gain additional value from certain packaging of the content (such as narrating/licensing an audio version, for those who want to listen to the content instead of reading it), or the author may be asked to participate in consultation/conferences about the topic the book covers, in return for some compensation.

And fans like physical manifestations of their media; for years, rock concerts weren't designed to profit strictly from ticket sales—a concert tour was meant to stimulate interest and increase sales of ancillary materials. Yes, this included recordings of the music, but it's also about merchandising (gotta have that T-shirt with the name of the band on it), food and beverage, exclusive access, and perhaps a copy of the recorded media with the creator's signature on it. Universal access to data does not eliminate all potential revenue streams for the content creators, producers, and distributors.

Unchill

There's another massively beneficial aspect to greater transparency, again from the production side: the destruction of the chilling effect.

In recent years, the chilling effect has emerged not as the result of government censorship and regulation, but as market reaction to social cues. Members of the public have expressed outrage about certain artistic works to the point where the content creators/publishers have suspended, delayed, or halted production of the work . . . sometimes before the work has even been publicly released.[16][17]

In our quasi-private world, one of the most befuddling facets of cancel culture is that those members of the public calling for a creative work to be halted are sometimes anonymous, and their motives questionable. For instance, critics of a pending work might also be content creators themselves, begging the question whether it is truly the new content

---

[16]reason.com/2020/01/17/canceled-transgender-story
[17]reason.com/2019/12/31/cancel-culture-2019-year

they find disagreeable or whether it's the competition for audience they are resisting, or even whether their vocal disparaging of the new work is simply an opportunity for self-aggrandizement and publicity. If we (everyone) don't know their (the critics') identity, intent, and total other activities, we have no way of judging whether their critique is forthright and sincere or hypocritical and opportunistic.

With total transparency, we'll be able to see for ourselves just who is calling for content to be limited, and why. More importantly, we'll see if someone who describes a work as racist, jingoistic, misogynistic, or having any other popularly negative shortcoming, comports themselves, in their day-to-day life, in accordance to the same standard for which they hold those creators they're accusing.

And, most important of all, with total transparency and lack of hindrances on data distribution, voices cannot be stifled by either statute or outrage (feigned or felt). I don't *need* to find a publisher for a book I want to write: I can reach a global audience, today, by self-publishing online. Anyone who writes anything can find an audience, large or small, among the totality of readers worldwide. The same can be said for almost any form of personal expression: current technology affords us the opportunity to share a film, song, painting, or software application instantly, at extremely low (or no) cost.

This is true even when one outlet may choose to decide to cease publication of certain content; as one portal shuts down, other competing portals open wide. When Google subsidiary YouTube decided to cease revenue-sharing for video content that featured certain aspects of firearms,[18] firearm-related content creators were welcomed by another large, popular, secure host of video content: PornHub.[19]

In a world with truly open access, not only the audience benefits, but the content creators, as well; the chilling effect is dissipated, whether the source was a government censor, a shrill anonymous voice, or a reactionary publisher/content distributor. Humanity wins.

Troll Toll?

Of course, critics with a political bent are not the only groups intent on affecting conversations in what may be a negative way. There are also

---

[18]support.google.com/youtube/answer/7667605
[19]www.pewpewtactical.com/youtube-firearms-alternatives

people who enjoy disrupting order and tweaking more delicate sensibilities: these people do it for the lulz.

It's an ancient hobby: find whatever ideals, perspectives, or manners are currently held sacred and then do/say the opposite. If you can tilt the opposition (often just normal people) into overreacting, responding in outrage, or contradicting their own rules, you get bonus points. Children do it instinctually; adults can do it for effect.

Gandhi did it.[20] Voltaire did it.[21] Ben Franklin did it.[22] Socrates really committed to the bit.[23]

It's another way to morph conversation, to challenge ideals and determine whether other people are acting in a principled manner, or to feign seriousness as a means of self-aggrandizement or perceived importance. It's a form of civil disobedience and entertainment.

A good example is from 2016, when the UK's Natural Environmental Research Council (NERC) held an online poll as a promotional activity;

---

[20]Among other wonderful moments of trolling, Gandhi notified British authorities that he purposefully intended to make a public demonstration of violating the law against Indians producing their own salt; he publicized his request and made a great show of the illegal acts, provoking the British colonial government into overreacting against him and his followers. www.thoughtco.com/what-was-gandhis-salt-march-195475

[21]In "Candide," Voltaire used satire to attack the ruling class of his day; he skewers philosophers, the aristocracy, the military, and religion. It was very daring for its time, and still very funny today. Just go read it. It's in the public domain, and you can find free copies on the Internet.

[22]In his autobiography (cleverly titled *The Autobiography of Benjamin Franklin*) Franklin explains that he could not get published in his brother's newspaper under his own name, so he delivered letters to the paper with the signature, "Silence Dogood." Fourteen of these letters were eventually published, and Franklin created an elaborate backstory for his pseudonymous character. Under the nom de plume, Franklin pretended to complain about all sorts of topics, including hoop skirts and dating. franklinpapers.org/framedVolumes.jsp

[23]According to Plato (in his *Apology*), Socrates referred to himself as a "gadfly," intending to irritate and annoy the state in which he lived, sometimes out of belief of his own utterances, but sometimes because (so Socrates believed) it is important to challenge even the most cherished ideals. He made a point of approaching people who were publicly viewed as "wise," and questioning them about their beliefs in order to prove that their "knowledge" had no logical or value basis. Eventually, Socrates angered enough important people to receive a death sentence (he was forced to drink poison); when offered opportunities to escape his fate, he chose to comply with the state's orders, instead. classics.mit.edu/Plato/apology.1b.txt [Yes, the link goes to a text file with no formatting; this is a form of trolling, and driving home the earlier point about data format having value.]

the poll asked for public participation in naming NERC ship, a research vessel.[24] People a were asked to suggest names or to vote on suggestions that others had made.

The name with the most votes, the winner, was Boaty McBoatface.

This is funny on several levels. The name itself is comical; it's the sort of thing a child would come up with. The words have a certain inherent, whimsical sound. Also, naming an oceangoing craft with a mission many people consider important (scientific investigation) in the manner that a toy or cartoon mascot might be named creates a mental dichotomy (purpose of the thing: adult/name of the thing: childish).

The NERC was forced into a rather odd position: accept the popular winner of the poll or reveal the action as a rather crass form of corporate promotion, in which the organization was only aping a populist intent, but not truly willing to accept the democratic outcome.

The NERC chose to name the boat "RRS Sir David Attenborough."[25]

The British have a slang term for this sort of activity: taking the piss [out of]. It's a time-honored practice (the term has been around for decades, if not centuries); satire/parody are a form of taking the piss. Anyone who mocks a self-important institution or person is taking the piss out of the target. Taking the piss is especially respected when it is performed in deadpan so that the sarcastic intent might not be immediately recognized and might be misconstrued as agreement/camaraderie with the target.

In modern online parlance, this is called *trolling*.[26] The troll doesn't believe the assertion (often a counterargument to a given consensus); the troll wants to evoke dramatic results from the in-group, often

---

[24]The poll originally existed at this website but has since been taken down: nameour-ship.nerc.ac.uk/entries.html

[25]In a hilarious follow-up, a man named Gary Jackson created an online petition asking Attenborough to change *his* name to "Boaty McBoatface," so that the ship would have to likewise be renamed. www.itv.com/news/2016-05-08/petition-for-david-attenborough-to-be-renamed-boaty-mcboatface

[26]The term *trolling* is often used to describe other types of behavior, to the point where someone may use it to mean, "any kind of online activity I don't like." In this way, it has taken on an amorphous, negative connotation, much like the terms *harassment* and *bullying*—nobody wants to be an advocate *for* harassment or bullying, but the words have been applied to so many actions, including innocuous activity, that they no longer have the impact/importance they once had.

to highlight hypocrisy, expose elitism, or simply deflate self-importance.[27]

Without privacy, trolling might be reduced; quite often, the troll relies on Internet anonymity to conduct the trolling. Not many people want to be known as the person who entered a vegan forum online only to post photos of cow corpses in a slaughterhouse along with the text, "HAHA! Meet Tastes Good, Veggie Whiners!!1!1!!! #vegetablessuck" (or something more racially/ethnically charged). Privacy affords the troll the comfort to launch the drama-attack. When your parents, employer, colleagues, clients, and friends can all see that *you* have written/done something, you may be more inclined to behave politely.

Given the opportunity, I'd still vote for "Boaty McBoatface," though.

Another practice that may be dramatically reduced in a totally transparent world is *doxing*: revealing the personal details of someone's life (home address, phone number, email address, employer's contact information, etc.). This is a perennial favorite of online vigilantes and activists. It depends, however, on the target's desire for privacy. If there's nothing to be revealed, then there's no negative impact in doxing—it doesn't serve as a threat or punishment.

Might transparency in this manner—knowing someone's personal contact information—exacerbate the potential misuse of that information? If everyone knows someone's email address, phone number, home address, etc., might that lead to the person receiving personal threats and verbal/written attacks? I don't think so . . . because transparency would also reveal the people making the threats/attacks, as well. And any threat that implies actual violence or communication escalating to harassment is already a crime (and should be prosecuted as such), and rational members of society are not going to tolerate someone acting in such an egregious manner.

Moreover, if I *know* who is making threats or harassing me, I can choose to block that person's communication. I can even recommend that others block that person, too. In a world with complete information access, I will even know when that person uses a different phone line

---

[27]What *South Park* would deem "super cereal": someone who believes their own cause is so overwhelmingly important that everyone else (whether they agree with the cause or not) must be forced to make it a priority and treat it with respect. southpark.cc.com/full-episodes/s10e06-manbearpig

or new email address to try to reach me . . . and I can block that communication, too.

The Threat of Erasure

This does, however, create a new potential problem: virtual erasure. If someone does something that many people do not like, and many people block that person's communication, and many *other* people trust the block inherently, and also the block the target, the person who is blocked may be unable to function in a modern society.

Effectively, this would ostracize the person, making them an outcast and severely limiting their ability to function in a connected world.

This type of erasure could create a subclass of outcasts—people unable to avail themselves of a "normal" life in a tech-heavy culture. They might become invisible to others around them, because the Erased would have no online presence . . . and no ability to undo the Erasure. How do you tell people you've reformed, if people are no longer listening to you, and cannot even hear what you're saying? How do you demonstrate the change in your character if you aren't being seen?

I'm not just referring to social circles, either; this goes beyond losing friends or acquaintances, or the luxury of being connected online. What if Erased people have trouble getting employment or access to services or even establishing their identity? I wrote earlier in the book about the difficulty of basic lifestyle capabilities (renting lodging, getting hired, making purchases) while attempting anonymity. What if that anonymity is forced upon you? What if you can't reclaim your identity, because your identity has been tainted irredeemably?

Maybe *that* would even become a commercial or systemic service in a transparent world: subscription to a monitoring agency that rechecks Erased individuals to determine if they've modified their behavior or an insurance policy for yourself in case you get Erased or a company that offers to help you repair your identity in case of Erasure (as credit-repair agencies do now). All of these things could also, of course, quite easily become a social ill; there are many science fiction stories that feature the perils of a social-rating system that manifests a rather ugly dystopia.[28]

---

[28]An excellent episode of *Black Mirror* predicated the implementation of an actual social credit system in China: apnews.com/9d43f4b74260411797043ddd391c13d8

Get Out

There's one aspect of privacy I haven't touched on in the rest of the book, one more way we use it in our quasi-private world today: transparency will remove privacy in voting.

Secret voting is stupid. And anti-democratic. The sooner we get rid of it, the better.

The typical justification for maintaining privacy in elections is that it will discourage despots; if the ballot box is sacrosanct, then no individual can be punished by the ruling class for making the "wrong" choice, and voters can punish rulers as they see fit.[29]

Perhaps. But secret voting has never seemed to prevent totalitarian regimes from existing; in fact, if ballots are secret and there is no attribution to individual voters, nobody has any real way to ensure votes were cast in accordance with the voters' wishes.[30] In the current quasi-private environment, election "monitors" enforce personal security at ballots, ensuring voters can reach polls, can cast votes without interference, and that the ballots collected in the poll boxes are tabulated, but there's no way of completely ensuring the ballots themselves are utterly secure (for instance, monitors can't be sure that voters aren't under threat/coercion prior to arriving or after leaving the polling place).

Moreover, even in countries where open polling does not require physical security to protect voters, there are historical precedents for traditions of all sorts of election interference, such as buying votes, ballot-stuffing, and "lost" ballots (I grew up near Chicago and currently live

---

[29]Another reason that is sometimes suggested to support secret ballots is to avoid the possibility of quid pro quo voting, or "buying" votes. This is a fairly recent phenomenon/justification. The founders of the United States had no such qualms about the practice of rewarding votes; George Washington used the tactic during an election: "During his campaign, he supplied voters with 28 gallons of rum, 50 gallons of rum punch, and 82 gallons of wine, beer, and cider." www.mountvernon.org/library/digitalhistory/digital-encyclopedia/article/rum
The idea that politicians should not be allowed to "buy" votes is comical to the modern electorate, who are quite used to politicians promising to fund the pet projects of various voting blocs (or individual voters) on a constant basis. American elections are a spoils system that secret balloting has not deterred, so the benefit of secrecy is negligible at best.
[30] Saddam Hussein retained power for his despotism during referenda in 1995 and 2002, when he won 99.96 percent and 100 percent of the votes, respectively. www.cbsnews.com/news/saddam-hussein-wins-one-man-race

in Louisiana; in both places, a "fair" election is a thing of legends and myth). Would (and should) we really trust a process that is administered by volunteers and elected bureaucrats?

So secret ballots are worse than pointless; they are susceptible to corruption and scamming.

We don't use that process anywhere else, in either politics or business; every other time we vote, whether as an elected member of the US Senate or as a minor shareholder electing the Board of Directors of a corporation, our name and position is attributed to our vote—we take responsibility and accountability for our decision.

I want that. Of all the things I've described in this book, this is the one outcome of ending privacy that I look forward to and doesn't terrify me. I want to know if my neighbors attempt to force me to pay for something or try to abrogate my freedoms—if someone I know wants to limit, say, my ability to engage in hobbies such as gambling, smoking tobacco products, eating desserts, riding a motorcycle, or drinking alcohol, then I want that person to express their desire, exerted through elections and referenda, clearly and with purpose. If a voter wants to interfere with another person's sexual relationships, human rights, or business, then we should all know the name of that voter.

If you *truly believe* you have the right to exert force against someone else for a specific reason, then you should have the moral conviction to stand by your assertion and frankly state your intent, *regardless of the effects*.

Yes, I will definitely punish someone for what I think is a "bad" vote; if the owner of a local grocery store tries to prevent me from reading a book I want to read, I am going to stop shopping at that grocery. If my neighbor tries to prevent me from having whiskey when I want it, I'm not going to bring my neighbor's trash can up from the street on garbage pick-up day as a courtesy. I will not initiate physical force against anyone for their choice at the polls, but I certainly won't be kind to them or reward them in any way.

We don't *need* privacy for conducting democratic elections. In fact, democracy will be much better off without it.

On the Genetic Level

I've briefly mentioned that the ubiquity of genetic analysis capabilities is reducing privacy and enhancing transparency. It's worth mentioning just a few potential benefits (and risks) associated with these developments.

The obvious risks are the dissipation of cherished illusions and clannish myths: regardless of the family stories you've been told, you can already know your lineage accurately, which may cause discomfort for some of the people who'd rather you didn't. This may also cause discomfort for some of the people who also did not know the truth—discomfort of the legal, financial, and emotional variety.

Here's just one wild example: you find out you have a medical condition that requires a treatment that includes a transfusion or transplant; you also find out you have no immediate family members who share the particular genetic traits necessary for the treatment. You locate someone who doesn't even know they are related to you, and approach them asking for a life-saving contribution of flesh/blood. Should they feel obligated to donate? What if the extraction procedure is life-threatening (or even just life-shortening)?

Carried a step further, we can approach dystopian outcomes again: what if your genetic sequence maps your entire future— how smart you are, how healthy you are, your lifespan, etc.? The film *Gattaca* is immensely entertaining and posits just such a society: every person is pigeonholed from the moment of conception.

However, the benefits of full personal knowledge and data transparency almost assuredly outweigh the fictional risks. Aside from the moral value of the truth versus convenient myth, if I know as much about myself as possible, data I can share with my medical providers to seek and acquire treatment, I can conceivably enhance and extend my life far beyond whatever random approach I might have taken in the absence of that knowledge. If I am deathly allergic to peanuts, I'd like to know that before munching on that first (and last) candy bar.

Going back to the donor scenario: what if the person being approached by the genetic match was willing to suffer discomfort and possible health impacts in order to save another human life? Right now, most jurisdictions outlaw any sort of reward or financial incentive for life-saving donation of biological material. Even without that motivation, what if the donor was willing to contribute out of a sense of nobility and kindness? But . . . what if the donor didn't know they *were* a potential donor? Not hypothetical, but completely anecdotal: I had a cousin who died of leukemia at the age of 18, mainly because her genetic lineage was so rare that not many similar donors existed to provide the marrow that could have saved her life (more than 70,000 people contacted the donor registry to offer to contribute; most were disqualified as matches even before testing their marrow).[31]

Transparency could save and enhance lives. It may also cause pain, expense, and moral quandaries. I'd still rather have the knowledge.

Still Scared

Writing a book like this is basically putting a big target on your back: "please come reveal all my data, show everyone my slightest hypocrisy, expose my every moral failing and human shortcoming." Just pointing out that openness and transparency might not be the evil we expect, and that there may be some benefit, will be, to some audiences, tantamount to advocating for a dystopian police surveillance state. There will be those among those audiences who loathe me for saying these things and those who wish to do me harm. Some of these will find it amusingly equitable and a form of justice to expose me and dox me, because of how I've couched my arguments.

And some of them, maybe just even a very few, will have the capacity to do so.

It's going to be awkward for many of us, transitioning from the current quasi-private world into one of full transparency. This will be especially true for those of us who are older, and even more true for those jurisdictions that try to fight the inevitable leap into total access by imposing regulation and restriction. In those places, in fact, I expect there to be significant violence and upheaval that go beyond just the emotional strife and embarrassment exposure will cause everyone.

Even the nonviolent transitions will entail immeasurable pain. We're already beginning to see what the truth can do when deep lies are exposed: as home genetic services become more ubiquitous, lies about lineage and origin and relationships are exploding, and families/businesses/lives are being ripped apart. That's bad—pain and misery are never good.

But . . .

Is that pain and misery better or worse than a lie that prevents you from knowledge of your true DNA . . . and perhaps keeps you from seeking or finding medical attention for a specific condition you would

---

[31]www.fredhutch.org/en/news/center-news/2014/01/rod-carew--striking-out-cancer.html

have known about if you hadn't been lied to for generations? Is it better to live with pain and misery or die due to lies?

I've got genetic Jewish and gypsy and Polish and Italian content in my cells; knowing that may allow me to detect Tay-Sachs complications if I ever chose to have children. It also allows a potential romantic partner to discriminate against me in a dating pool, if the one thing the partner seeks (and prizes most highly) is uncomplicated reproduction. Transparency benefit: I know the medical risks. Transparency cost: so does everyone else.

Total access will not cure all societal ills; in fact, it will exacerbate some, and the transition from here to there will be incredibly painful. But ending privacy is also not the definite recipe for dystopia we may have been led to believe, either.

I'm looking forward to knowing you on the other side.

Index